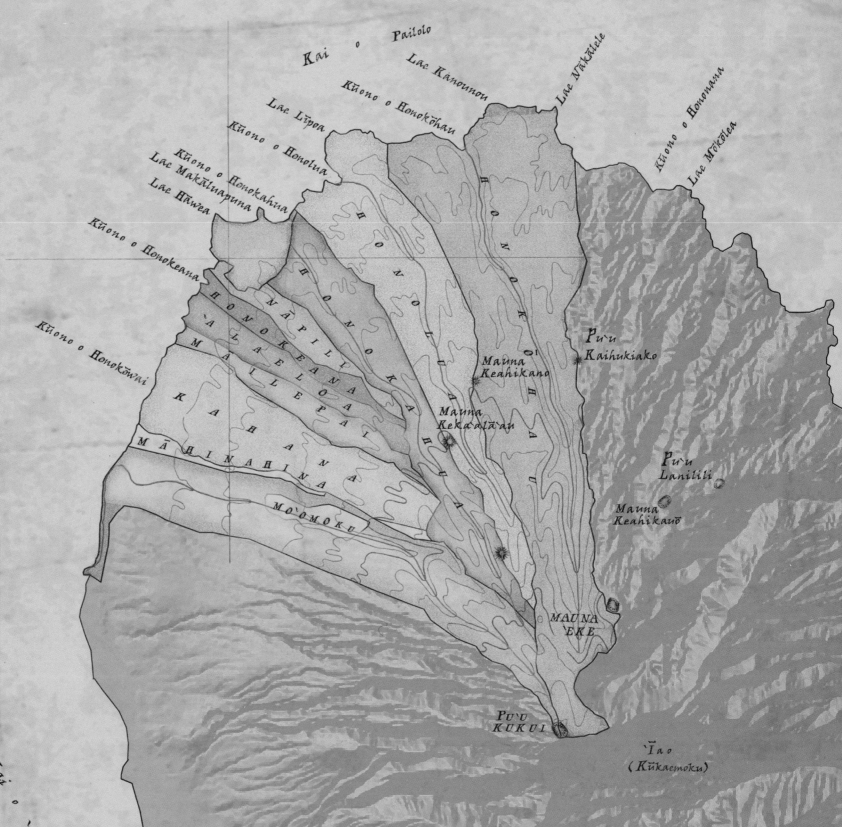

Kai o Pailolo

Lae Kanounou

Lae Nākālele

Kūono o Honokōhau

Lae Lipoa

Kūono o Hononana

Kūono o Honolua

Lae Mōkōlea

Kūono o Honokahua

Lae Makāluapuna

Lae Hāwea

Kūono o Honokeana

H
O
N
O
K
Ō
H
A
U

H
O
N
O
L
U
A

Kūono o Honokōwai

NĀPILI

HONOKEANA

'ALAELOA

KAHANA

HONOKŌWAI

Mauna
Keahikano

Pu'u
Kaihukiako

Mauna
Keka'alā'au

MĀHINAHINA

Pu'u
Lanilili

Mauna
Keahikauō

MO'OMOKU

MAUNA
EKE

PU'U
KUKUI

'Īao
(Kūkaemoku)

Kai o 'Au'au

William Horak October 2007

Kapalua Nui

PLACE OF LIFE

Jocelyn Fujii

HULA MOON PRESS, LLC

O Kuʻu ʻĀina ʻO Honokahua

ʻO kuʻu ʻāina one hānau…kuʻu ʻāina o nā ʻōiwi
Beloved sands of my birth…land of ancestors long passed

ʻO kuʻu ʻāina wā kamaliʻi…kuʻu ʻāina leʻaleʻa
Land of my childhood years…a place of simple joy

ʻO kuʻu ʻāina o nā kānaka…kuʻu ʻāina pūliki ʻia
Land thriving with common heritage…a place which embraces

ʻO kuʻu ʻāina o nā mākua…kuʻu ʻāina ikaika ia
Land of my parents, one of strength and honor

ʻO kuʻu ʻāina home kūpuna…kuʻu ʻāina hoʻomaha
Land of those from whom I descend, where I find restful peace

ʻO kuʻu ʻāina pili puʻuwai…kuʻu ʻāina poina ʻole
Land at the very heart of my life, one that I will never forget

ʻO kuʻu ʻāina haliʻa…kuʻu ʻāina ʻo Honokahua ma Kapalua
Always in mind and memory, Honokahua at Kapalua

E ola…e ola…e ola ʻo Honokahua
May you always live on…live on…Honokahua

—Piʻimauna ʻAiwohi

Kapalua

Kapalua Nui
Place of Life

By Jocelyn Fujii

Copyright © 2008 Hula Moon Press
First edition, 2008

Photographs © Maui Land & Pineapple Company, Inc., with the
exception of the following:
© Franco Salmoiraghi, page 23
© Ben Young, page 50, left

Maps © William Horak and © Hula Moon Press

Except where noted on page 106, photographs are courtesy the
archives of Maui Land & Pineapple Company, Inc., and the photo
library of Kapalua Marketing.

Library of Congress Control Number: 2007935267
ISBN 978-0-9794649-1-1

Cover photograph by Bob Bangerter
Map design by William Horak, horakbbt@comcast.net

Printed in Singapore

Contents

Foreword

When I was eleven years old, my parents organized a family excursion to the Valley Isle that ultimately led to my first impressions of West Maui. We began our journey on a narrow road along the treacherous Pali, my father offering sound effects at every turn to the screams and delight of my younger siblings. Then, as we rounded Papawai Point, another island came into view. Not a tiny offshore island like those we knew so well back home in Kailua, but a looming, mountainous land mass sporting cliffs and courting its own clouds. Farther along the road, another more imposing island came into view, and I knew for the first time in my young life that I was part of a community of islands.

Today I know Lāna'i and Moloka'i as part of Maui Nui and the familiar western vista of Kapalua Nui. After several years of celebrating the sunsets from Kapalua Bay, I can fix the time of year by observing where the sun touches the sea between our island sisters. The Kapalua Sundial.

Above Kapalua Bay in the distance lies Pu'u 'Eke, where scarce native plants thrive in unspoiled isolation. On this summit, and nowhere else in the world, grow miniature 'āhinahina, kin to Haleakalā's silverswords. This is a *wao akua*, considered by Hawaiians to be a sacred place of great *mana*.

Beyond the majestic beauty and intrinsic power of Kapalua Nui, there are extraordinary people who give this place its character and serve as our collective memory. Jocelyn Fujii brings the story of this place and its people to you in these pages and rekindles the sense of wonder we had as children for our natural world.

While that natural world is still vibrantly alive at Kapalua Nui, we recognize its frailties and strive to keep our human presence in proper perspective while planning the future.

Mankind's attempt to refashion the earth has intensified in recent history. Gone is the sense of interdependence and inter-reliance that we once knew in our daily lives. As stewards of Kapalua Nui, we are acutely aware of our duty to safeguard ancient traditions as well as the *'āina*. But we also know that it is only through conscious commerce that we can sustain the people who care for this place.

For over 100 years, the women and men of Maui Land & Pineapple Company have worked with our island community in shaping a harmonious culture. Building upon the pillars of the past, we have a strong foundation to support our efforts as we plant the seeds for the next 100 years. I hope you find nourishment in our traditions, environment, and lifestyle, and that you, too, will treasure our beloved home as a *Place of Life*.

I mua.

David C. Cole

Chairman, President and CEO
Maui Land & Pineapple Company, Inc.

Introduction

We have known it for years as Kapalua Resort. It came into our lives in 1978, when the Kapalua Bay Hotel opened its doors on a secluded bay in West Maui. It redefined our notions of green: the light, mossy hues of the surrounding fields of pineapple, luminous in morning light. The dark emerald of Cook pines as they wend across the landscape in orderly rows. The sensuous contours of the mauka lands, sloping seaward from Pu'u Kukui, the summit of the West Maui Mountains. And the bays, coves, and beaches—so many of them, each one different from the next, indulging us with their invitations. Pineapple fields seemed an unlikely backdrop for a luxurious resort community, but the hotel changed our perceptions of many things.

Thirty years later, a new era emerges. The original hotel is no more, but Kapalua, the resort community it seeded, takes flight with a new vision. The resort and its surroundings stand alone as the most spacious in Hawai'i, and among the largest in the world—on the scale of a national park. When the renaissance of the resort is completed and the master plan fulfilled, only a very small percentage of Kapalua Nui's 23,000 acres will have been developed.

In this book, we focus on the three major *ahupua'a*, the traditional Hawaiian land units, which form the nucleus of Kapalua Nui: Honokahua, Honolua, and Honokōhau, each endowed in different ways with natural beauty and cultural heritage. People of multiple generations and ethnicities reflect and share their stories of life in the plantation camps, their prickly summers in the cannery, and their carefree adventures in the mountains and at the shoreline. We see how punishing work and a gentle environment have shaped a culture that stayed loyal to its roots. We revisit pivotal events that occurred at Kapalua Nui and changed Hawai'i's history, from the launching of the voyaging canoe *Hōkūle'a* to the unprecedented relocation of The Ritz-Carlton, Kapalua to accommodate a sacred Hawaiian burial site. We see how an insular plantation community, with its origins in the late 1800s, builds on its heritage and makes its way in an increasingly global world. In these 23,000 acres of West Maui, something unprecedented is happening: the traditional dualities of local and global, visitor and resident, past and future, and growth and conservation are one.

Guiding the resort is the agricultural imprint that has always defined Maui Land & Pineapple Company. Organic community gardens, an organically managed farm, and a weekly farmer's market are the crux of the culinary life, whether at home or dining out. Plantation-style architecture in Honolua village honors a legacy with style. Open space soothes the senses, and the nature preserve of Pu'u Kukui goes counter to the norm by acquiring new land and native species. Recreation assumes new forms in the mountains and at the shoreline, and fresh amenities and services strive to balance access and preservation. Wellness, sustainability, "entrepreneurial agriculture"—words rarely heard in the plantation era—are spoken with conviction, pointing to the village of the future.

While every community is a reflection of its people, location is also paramount. West Maui's proximity to two islands across two channels gives it a unique perspective on the world. With Lāna'i eight miles away and Moloka'i a half-mile closer, what is a symbol of isolation to most—the horizon—is here the embodiment of relationship. More than a few newcomers have had this epiphany on their trips to West Maui, where the splendid sight of the islands offshore is surprisingly comforting and reassuring. From most shorelines in Hawai'i, views of the horizon are stark, infinite, and formless, suggesting a vast existential isolation. At Kapalua Resort, the sight of close-knit geologic forms, silent, stately siblings across narrow ocean channels, is not only aesthetically pleasing. It elevates our sense of community. And it hones our perceptions of ocean, land, and place in an increasingly hectic world.

Jocelyn Fujii

Ancient
MURMURS

Preceding page: A sunset view from Kapalua Bay looks out upon Lāna'i and Moloka'i. *This page:* A *mauka* view of Kapalua Resort reveals a scalloped shoreline and the Bays of Pi'ilani.

At the northern end of West Maui, as if the land were grasping the ocean with fingers stretched wide, six storied bays form a scalloped edge to the coast. Named after the celebrated chief who unified Maui in the 1500s, the bays form deep, colorful recesses that add a dramatic border to the land. They are called Nā Hono a Pi'ilani: the Bays of Pi'ilani.[1] Their names roll off the tongue with a rhythm all their own: Honokōwai, Honokeana, Honokahua, Honolua, Honokōhau, Hononana.[2] As the bays appear and disappear along the curves of Honoapi'ilani Highway, the road narrows, the air softens, and the islands of Lāna'i and Moloka'i loom closer across the channels.

The character of the shoreline changes around every corner, from the sandy openness of Honokahua Bay to the stark sea cliffs of reef-rich Honolua. The air becomes cooler, fed by the trade winds of the Pailolo Channel. Sharp, flat points of land alternate with cliffs above beaches of sand and pebbles where wedge-tailed shearwaters soar overhead. The road curls, and a blowhole wheezes near Nākālele Point. Inland, beyond sight, deep in the folds of Honokōhau Valley, one of the world's tallest waterfalls plunges 1,700 feet to the valley floor.[3] When the eye moves *mauka*, a soothing green patchwork bespeaks a land as fertile as the sea. Valleys incise the landscape, calling to mind a time when terraces of taro sustained communities of Hawaiians who lived off the land, fished in the bays, and gathered stone and fiber plants for their dwellings.

This is the rounded northern edge of the west coast of Maui, a paean to the glories of geology and nature. Known as the "Haven of Pi'ilani," larger in size than O'ahu and second to the island of Hawai'i, Maui is shaped like the upper body of a woman.[4] As seen on a map, her head points west, her chin juts south, and her waistline tapers to the east. At the crown of her head is a fan-shaped swath of 23,000 acres, larger than many national parks and nearly one-fourth the size of Lāna'i across the channel. These are the lands that make up Kapalua Nui, a towering physical and cultural presence in the district of Kā'anapali, one of the twelve *moku* of the island.[5]

Old-timers know it by the names of its valleys, streams, and *ahupua'a*, the traditional Hawaiian land division around which community life revolved. Kapalua Nui is a neatly stitched patchwork of ten contiguous ahupua'a, long, graceful wedges that sweep from the heights of Mauna Kahalawai, the West Maui Mountains, to the west and northwest coasts.[6]

Wider at the ocean and narrowing toward the mountain, the ahupua'a of old comprised an ingenious system of land and ocean management that began in the mountains and extended beyond the outer reefs. It encompassed terrestrial, freshwater, and ocean resources and was a well-managed system of ecology, economics, agriculture, and aquaculture for Hawaiians. In the valleys of Honokahua, Honolua, and Honokōhau— the nucleus of Kapalua Resort—abundant *lo'i*, taro fields, were fed by streams from the upland watershed that sustained communities of Hawaiians in times past.

It is thought that Honokōhau alone contained the most extensive system of taro cultivation on this coast.[7] From salt at the shore to taro in the wetlands to timber on the higher slopes, the Hawaiians gathered their necessities in an efficient system of sharing and exchange up and down the ahupua'a: wood for canoes and structures, bark for cloth, *kukui* for lighting and medicine, stone for walls and temples, thatch for homes, plants and fish for food.

The mother of this land is Mauna Kahalawai, the fertile mountain range that defines West Maui. Its slopes are sharply chiseled, spawning chasms, valleys, and streams in their journey seaward from the summit. Pu'u Kukui, the "Hill of Light," is Kahalawai's summit, a commanding presence some 5,788 feet above sea level, shrouded in mist in the lofty heart of West Maui. From the heights of this volcano, a peerless treasure emerges: the Pu'u Kukui Watershed Preserve, Hawai'i's largest private nature preserve and one of the most biologically rich regions in the state. Where the mountain meets the shoreline, amid Pi'ilani's vaunted namesakes, two stellar bays, Mokulē'ia and Honolua, compose the Honolua-Mokulē'ia Marine Life Conservation District, teeming with life in reef-rich waters. Visible from the shoreline, across the 'Au'au and Pailolo channels, the islands of Lāna'i and Moloka'i glow green and purple in the changing light, their volcanic forms dreamlike in the vast oceanic canvas.

One can only imagine what Pi'ilani and the chiefs of old thought of these lands as they crossed the ocean channels, walked the contours of the ahupua'a, and

Preceding page: Honolua Ridge has the classic features of the *ahupua'a*, a traditional Hawaiian land unit stretching from mountain to ocean.

discovered the extremities of their own unique world. Looking mauka to the heights of Mauna Kahalawai and seaward to Lāna'i and Moloka'i, one ponders the powers that created them. Nearly one-and-a-half million years ago, Kahalawai, and later Haleakalā, emerged from the sea as two discrete volcanic cones. As their lava flows connected through the eons, layer upon layer, the isthmus of central Maui took shape, and the volcanoes merged into one formidable island: Maui Nui. Slowly and relentlessly, succumbing to the forces of erosion, wind, waves, and fluctuating sea levels, Moloka'i, Lāna'i, and Kaho'olawe eventually separated from Maui Nui, and a family of islands, later to become known as Maui Nui a Kama, was born.[8]

Mythic tales celebrate the sisterhood of these islands in the vivid, often hyperbolic recounting of Hawai'i's oral tradition. Kiha-a-Pi'ilani, the son of Pi'ilani, is said to have surfed from this region of West Maui to Moloka'i across the Pailolo Channel. "On this sailing of the canoes with the chiefs and the commoners for Molokai, the ocean was completely covered with canoes from Ka'anapali to Waialua on Molokai," wrote Elspeth Sterling in *Sites of Maui*, quoting a story by Moses Manu in *Ka Nupepa Kuokoa*.[9] "As for the chief, Kihapiilani, he did not board any canoe but rode a long surfboard from Honolua and the wild surging waves of the Pailolo Sea carried him with difficulty, a deed by which the famous waves of that deep blue sea were turned into a plaything as well as a sport by that chief." There were lei on his head, Manu continued, but "not a particle of spray from the waves was seen tossing up over the adornment of leis on this chief, up to the time of his landing on the shore of Waialua on Molokai."

Kiha-a-Pi'ilani's feat held his observers in awe. "This was the very first time for the Ruling Chief who surfed on the long surf board from Maui to Molokai over the Sea of Pailolo, the sea which dashed to pieces the bodies of men from ancient times until this day," Manu concluded.

As the ocean claimed its share of human life, so did the frequent battles among the chiefs of the archipelago.

Early accounts of northwest Maui, of the Kapalua Nui area, are scarce. The pre-contact Hawaiians had an oral tradition passed on through the centuries, long before the missionaries brought the printed word with them in 1820. But even through the blank pages of history, it is known that the seductive power of Maui placed it high on the wish lists of the expansionist Hawaiian chiefs. The proximity of northwest Maui to Moloka'i across the Pailolo Channel made it more accessible and desirable in the lusty turf wars among the pre-contact chiefs.

"This place had importance in the history of Maui," noted cultural historian Kepā Maly, who has conducted historical and cultural research on the region. "Wherever we find place names, there are traditions and events in people's lives, natural phenomena, things that became valued to the people of the place. In the Kā'anapali region, the area from Honokōwai to Kahakuloa, there are interesting accounts pertaining to each place.

"In the later 1600s, we find accounts of canoes lining the coast from Lahaina through Kā'anapali— canoes from the warring invading fleets, preparing to go on their journeys, stretching across the entire coastline wherever canoes could be landed. The food resources made these lands exceptionally valued."

In his book *Ruling Chiefs of Hawaii*, the historian Samuel Kamakau describes battles on, for, and around the island—East Maui against West Maui, and Maui against Hawai'i Island—in the centuries before Kamehameha unified the Islands in the late 1700s. One saga before Kamehameha's reign involved a famous battle in West Maui in 1738. Kamehameha-nui, heir to the Maui kingdom, had been driven from Maui and was joined by his uncle, Alapa'i-nui, chief of Hawai'i. Together they returned to Maui to engage in battle against the usurpers, who were joined by Pele-io-holani of O'ahu. The strategy of Alapa'i-nui and Kamehameha-nui was to starve and weaken their opponents by drying up the irrigation systems and taro fields in Honokōwai, Wailuku, and parts of

Lahaina.[10] Upon hearing this, Pele-io-holani assembled his forces further north, in Honokahua and Honolua. Many warriors were killed in the battles that ensued along the coast of the district, but a truce was eventually reached, and Kamehameha-nui became chief of Maui once again.

"Although the chiefs were bound by blood and allegiance, disagreement and warfare divided them into victors and those vanquished," observed Carol Silva, historian and archivist with the Hawai'i State Archives. "Thus history is more an account of those who win and conquer; the stories of the defeated often perish with them on the field of battle. As a result, few details are known about Maui chiefs before they were ultimately defeated by Kamehameha in the eighteenth century."

The battles throughout the centuries proved that peace was only as enduring as the leanings of the prevailing ruler. But Pi'ilani was compassionate and just, the bringer of peace and stability who achieved immortality as much through his public works as through the oral history that commemorates him. He ruled from Hāna in East Maui to the bays of West Maui. The Bays of Pi'ilani, among the most magnificent in the state, confer honor upon him to this day. Renowned for his intelligence, Pi'ilani created order and prosperity and turned his chiefdom into a paradigm of enlightened government. He built the models for a sustainable life: fish ponds, irrigation systems, trails, and *heiau*, the pre-contact Hawaiian temples. He kept his court in West Maui's Lahaina and sought refuge in East Maui's Hāna, where he maintained his home and began construction on Hawai'i's largest heiau. Among Pi'ilani's enduring public works was the first phase of a trail that connected Maui's scattered Hawaiian settlements—the *alaloa*, "long road," also called Alanui Kīke'eke'e-a-Maui, the King's Highway.[11]

The alaloa was a major component of pre-contact village life, requiring monumental feats of masonry. Smooth stones were passed, hand-to-hand, across formidable distances to build a roadway wide enough, by some accounts, to accommodate eight of the king's warriors side by side. "There are only segments of the trail left, lined with rocks, solid, and all of them passed from hand to hand along long lines of common men," explained Lahaina kupuna Edna Pualani Farden Bekeart. "Imagine, they did this without the wheel, without the tools that we have today."

So efficient were these cobbled paths that they did not need to be widened when horses and carts were introduced to the island. The steeper grades required flatter stones, while the sloping country paths, more rounded stones. Large field boulders flanked the trails in open country terrain.[12] When Kiha-a-Pi'ilani, Pi'ilani's son, completed his father's network of roads in the 1500s, Maui achieved an unparalleled distinction. It became the only Hawaiian island to be completely girdled by an alaloa.[13]

"It was paved with stones along much of its extent, hence it was referred to as the 'Kipapa' (pavement) of Kihapi'ilani," noted E. S. Craighill Handy and Elizabeth Handy in *Native Planters in Old Hawaii*. "Beaches were used as crossings where gulches come down to the shore. There were no bridges, and beaches also were used along the seashore…Travelers were sometimes ferried across streams by canoe, or along shore…"[14] The alaloa eased not just travel; it was useful for the kings' messengers, the news-bearing *kūkini*, and for tax collectors and warriors.

While most of the alaloa has been obliterated by time or covered by modern construction, scattered remnants exist in and around Kapalua. One known remnant is recalled where the ahupua'a of Honokōhau meets neighboring Kahakuloa. "From Kahakuloa to Honokohau the old trail was turned into a horse trail," wrote the Handys. "Along the flatland east of Honokohau its route is no longer traceable." Quoting Martha Foss Fleming in *Old Trails of Maui*, they continued, "…it is in the best of condition as it winds down the steep pali near the ocean at Honokohau and after crossing the mouth of the stream shoots up the western pali."

Isao Nakagawa, a retired shop supervisor from Honolua Plantation and a former resident of Honolua Camp, recalled an impressive sight from his younger days: the Reverend John Kukahiko, minister of the Honokahua Congregational Church, traveling efficiently along the alaloa.[15] "Once a month, he would ride a horse from Honolua Camp to Kahakuloa following the alaloa," said Nakagawa with admiration. "And before the sun went down, he would be back. In one day. On a horse, on the old Hawaiian trail, this was fast." Nakagawa said he has traced the trail remnants nearly half the distance from Kapalua Resort to Kahakuloa, the ahupua'a north of the resort. "I can visualize where it went," he continued. "When you reach halfway to Kahakuloa, there's a beautiful, beautiful trail. It was real, almost intact. Before, in the 1960s, the trails were all intact until someone started to raise cattle there. The cattle started roaming and eating all the grass. The erosion started, and the trail was almost devastated."

"There were two remnants of alaloa on the Honokahua burial grounds and some remnants further north in the Nākālele Point area," added Richard Cameron, former vice president of property management for Maui Land & Pineapple Company and the son of Colin Cameron, its late president and chairman. Cameron was referring to the Honokahua Preservation Site on the grounds of The Ritz-Carlton, Kapalua, and Nākālele Point, adjacent to a landmark blowhole near the northernmost spot on the island.

"These were the clearest remnants. Past the blowhole, coming down in the valley, in an area where there were cattle, a couple of gullies with sections of alaloa could be seen." The two remnants he saw were modest, he said, "dozens of yards long rather than miles."

The stone remnants of heiau, the outdoor temples of pre-contact Hawaiians, are scattered throughout the ahupua'a of the Kapalua area, recalling times when larger communities of Hawaiians lived and planted in the valley. Heiau were ordered by the ruling class and usually faced the ocean from a promontory or commanding vantage point. They were built to

Next page: A rare segment of a pre-contact path, an *alaloa*, remains near the Honokahua Preservation Site.

honor the gods of the ocean, agriculture, war, and health, and to sanctify other aspects of Hawaiian life, including seasonal events and offerings. Wherever heiau are built, as in Kapalua Nui's Ili'ilikea Heiau and Maiu Heiau, they indicate a certain level of cultural significance.[16]

An archaeological survey of Ili'ilikea in 1992 revealed a complex structure encompassing a walled temple, a terraced temple, and supporting structures. Cattle ranching may have affected some of its features, such as a large enclosure found at the site. Despite the effects of ranching and erosion, the condition of the heiau was described as "good."[17]

Maiu Heiau, in the same valley, was noted by the archaeologist as "probably one of the last heiau to be dedicated on the island of Maui." Kamehameha II, Liholiho, dedicated it during a trip around Maui in 1819, and it was "intended as a site for human sacrifice."[18] A survey conducted in 1989 revealed platforms, terraces, walls, and enclosures among the forty-seven archaeological features discovered in the heiau.

Pre-contact finds such as these point to human habitation and activity, elements that historically evolve around abundant environmental resources: reasonable access; water for planting, drinking, and cleansing; ocean for fishing; soil for crops; materials for structures and canoes; stone for walls, foundations, and implements; and conditions conducive to recreation and ceremonial activities. The lands of Kapalua Nui had all these qualities and more, but just how extensively populated they were will never be conclusively known. In the first Mission Census for the Hawaiian Islands, reported in 1832 (fifty-four years after western contact), 728 Hawaiians were reported to be living in Kahakuloa and 2,982 in Kā'anapali.[19]

New revelations about early Hawaiian settlements came flooding to the surface in the late 1980s. When one of Hawai'i's most significant pre-contact burial sites was unearthed in the heart of Kapalua Resort, the birth pangs of a new cultural era rippled throughout the state.

The discovery took place in the sand dunes above Honokahua Bay, known today as D. T. Fleming Beach Park. Amid ironwoods on a knoll, where the sun can be seen rising over the eastern ridge of the bay, the excavation of the 5-acre site revealed bones of pre-contact Hawaiians within a 13.7-acre parcel designated for a Ritz-Carlton hotel. By the time the excavation ceased in December 1989, more than 1,012 sets of bones, dating back as far as 600 to the late 1800s AD, had been uncovered.[20] Declared the most significant site of its kind ever discovered in Hawai'i, it surprised historians and elevated Hawai'i's consciousness to new levels of cultural sensitivity.

"The old Hawaiian belief is that the spirit left the body at a place such as Honokahua and then travelled to a jumping-off point to leave earth and enter the spirit world," explained Caroline Peters Belsom, Native Hawaiian and vice president, general counsel for Kapalua Land Company, a wholly owned subsidiary of Maui Land & Pineapple Company. "The other possibility is that there might have been a fishing village there, as indicated by the artifacts. In those times, people would be buried on or near where they lived."

Ornaments and artifacts of shell, bone, boar tusk, shark teeth, wood, stone, and volcanic glass were among the findings at the site. Theresa Donham, the lead archaeologist for the project, suggested in her report that Honokahua "would have been well suited for permanent Hawaiian settlement."[21] Among the environmental features she described were excellent soil, a stream for irrigation, and ample rainfall, as well as extensive forest resources and "two protected bays with sand beaches for canoe landings.[22]

"The fact that there are traditional sites left at Honokahua is a strong testimony to the long history of Hawaiian presence in this area," she noted. "What remains is a small but very important portion of the traditional settlement system that was once present."

The Honokahua burial site became a lightning rod for what was a painful and important era in Hawai'i's cultural evolution. Led by a Maui group named Hui Alanui O Makena, protests by Hawaiian activists underscored their belief that a person's *mana*— spiritual power—resides after death in the bones and surrounding ground, making burial sites sacred and worthy of protection. After a period of negotiation involving Hawaiian, government, legal, and business interests, the late Colin Cameron, a fifth-generation *kama'āina* and then president and chairman of landowner Maui Land & Pineapple Company, signed an agreement ensuring "respectful and dignified treatment" of the *iwi*, the bones.[23]

The agreement, between Kapalua Land Company, the State Office of Historic Preservation, the Office of Hawaiian Affairs, and Hui Alanui O Makena, was the consummate example of a renaissance emerging out of tragedy. It allowed the state of Hawai'i to purchase the parcel and protect it forever as a cultural and historical treasure, the Honokahua Preservation Site. It called for the bones to be ceremoniously and respectfully returned to their original locations, or as close as possible. It required a strict protocol of documentation that resulted in heightened knowledge of the culture and social organization of pre-contact Hawaiians. And it led to the creation of important Native Hawaiian burial councils to monitor excavations

22

Indigenous elements include, *clockwise from top right*, a replica of a *pahu*, the drum of the ancients; terraces of taro; and the remnant of an *alaloa* from the reign of Pi'ilani and his son.

Lehua Pali, *left*, and Puanani Van Dorpe retrieve *kapa* from the Pali family lo'i, where natural elements have dyed the kapa black. The kapa was pounded by women for the reburials at Honokahua.

PUANANI VAN DORPE

The making of kapa for ceremonial purposes had not been attempted for centuries before the burials at Honokahua came to light. Because Hawaiian tradition calls for the bones to be wrapped in *kapa*, the bark cloth of the ancients, the prospect of reburying more than 1,000 iwi posed a challenge to the Hawaiian community.

Puanani Van Dorpe, a master unequalled in kapa-making, stepped forward and formed Hālau o Lauhuki me La'ahana, dedicated to the patron goddess of kapa. Thirteen women from throughout Hawai'i joined her, gathering daily in an old wooden house provided by Kapalua Land Company near the Honokahua burial site. Van Dorpe contributed her stored sheets of dried *wauke*, paper mulberry, which had been grown on Maui years earlier, and which Van Dorpe and her helpers from Lahainaluna School had harvested and scraped for a purpose then unknown. At Honokahua, the women of the hālau used stream water to re-awaken and soften the fibers, called bast. As they beat the bast into sheets, the sound of their wooden *i'e kuku* landing rhythmically on the anvils rang through the village like an ancient heartbeat.

Four months later, in March of 1990, the hālau finished making 1,012 sheets of kapa. As a special honor, Van Dorpe chose to dye every sheet black, the color for ali'i burials. For this, the women scraped the bark of kukui trees and used its blood-red juices to waterproof and strengthen the kapa. When dry, the kapa was taken to Honokōhau Valley, where Aimoku and Lehua Pali submerged each sheet in the mineral-rich mud of their lo'i. The chemical reaction of kukui juice interacting with sun and mud turned the kapa black in seven days.

Van Dorpe added a final touch: a watermark. On a special day on Moloka'i, at a kapa heiau that had been ceremonially re-opened for the occasion, Van Dorpe and the women of the hālau beat the watermark into seventeen sheets of black kapa. The watermark conferred a special distinction on the iwi that had been found with *lei niho palaoa*, carved hook-shaped pendants of bone and ivory, that indicate high rank.

The reburials were conducted in a solemn private ceremony at what is now the Honokahua Preservation Site. During the ceremony, witnesses reported seeing a Hawaiian short-eared owl, a *pueo*, circle overhead as whales sang in the bay below and clapped their fins on the water.

CLIFFORD NAE'OLE

Cultural Adviser, The Ritz-Carlton, Kapalua

The wind blows briskly upon the living sand dunes of the Honokahua Preservation Site. Countless grains of sand shift from one area of the dune to the other, creating a moving piece of art, a time capsule of culture. An ending brought a new beginning here. Pain brought new light. Many people— children and elders, commoners and ali'i—lived and died here, and left us their mana. The sanctity of this place brought an opportunity for Hawaiians to find deeper meaning in their heritage and ensure that their culture is not diluted. We have a covenant with the spirit of the land, and we proudly accept the responsibilities of stewardship. The *makani* (wind) represents the voice of our ancestors, and the *ua* (rain) symbolizes their touch. They truly bless this land and all who live here.

and discoveries of ancient burial sites on all of Hawai'i's islands. It was also agreed that the hotel would be relocated to accommodate the reinterment, a move that resulted in a different view and vantage point for the hotel.

Today the Honokahua Preservation Site is a tranquil patch of green surrounded by a *hau* hedge on a hill overlooking Moloka'i. Entry beyond the hedge is prohibited, and those who stop to read the plaque walk away with a feeling of tranquility and a renewed respect for Hawai'i's past. Honokahua has become a benchmark, a watershed of political and cultural consequence. The Hawaiians' respect for their *kūpuna*—their ancestors and elders—is upheld by the very presence of this historic site amid the changing faces of the modern world.

Every year at The Ritz-Carlton, Kapalua, the Celebration of the Arts, a Hawaiian cultural festival unparalleled in its authenticity, recognizes Hawai'i's host culture on lands that celebrate its presence daily. Clifford Nae'ole, cultural adviser for the hotel, conducts a year-round "Sense of Place" program that highlights the ethics and values imparted by the lessons of Honokahua.

"Kapalua is deeply committed to its sense of place," said Nae'ole. "And every single worker, employee, administrator, and executive of the resort comes here for cultural sensitivity training.

"Kapalua has become well-known because of the burials at Honokahua, and we respect that. We also have to remember that this happened here because the Hawaiians chose to live here. Everything was here— their families, their children, their kūpuna, the ocean, the water, all of the people and resources of daily life. Look around: it's beautiful. This was always a place to live, a place of life, where the entire circle of birth, life and death took place in the ahupua'a. It is a *leina 'uhane*, a never-ending cycle. The mana here is strong."

On Pineapple Hill, Cook pines capture a mood at sunset.

'Āina
ALOHA

Preceding page: Pu'u Kukui is a
towering beauty and the summit of
the West Maui Mountains. *This page:*
An *'ōhi'a* tree clings to a hillside in
the Pu'u Kukui Watershed Preserve.

Every mountain in the world has a summit, and Pu'u Kukui is one of them. But Pu'u Kukui is no ordinary mountaintop. Mantled in clouds some 5,788 feet above sea level, this remote summit of Mauna Kahalawai is the last frontier for some biological species that exist nowhere else in the world. Brooding and distant, with sharp edges and curtains of mist and rain, Pu'u Kukui was considered to be the meeting place of heaven and earth.

"The Hawaiians considered this area part of the *wao akua*, the God or Spirit Forest, of Mauna Kahalawai," explained Randy Bartlett, watershed manager for landowner Maui Land & Pineapple Company, Inc. (ML&P). "Our team at the Pu'u Kukui Watershed Preserve sees some of the best of what's left of the original, native Hawaiian flora and fauna that evolved in isolation for thousands of years—before any humans, including the first Polynesians, ever set foot on Maui's shores."

Pu'u Kukui is the visible landmark and highest point from which the West Maui land boundaries are determined, the single reference point that delineates the districts of Wailuku, Lahaina, and Kā'anapali. When measured through the interior of the island, the summit is two-and-a-half miles from its powerful counterpoint, 'Īao Needle, in the narrow neck of 'Īao Valley east of Pu'u Kukui.

From Pu'u Kukui, the "Hill of Light," flows an abundance of water, or *wai*—the Hawaiian word synonymous with wealth. Mauna Kahalawai denotes "the meeting or convergence of the waters," and the mountain lives up to its name.[1] Precipitation levels vary dramatically from the moist summit of the mountain—where the average annual rainfall is 360 inches but has been known to reach 600 inches in one year—to the sunny shores of Kapalua Resort, where swimmers and snorkelers cavort year-round.[2] The winds of Pu'u Kukui, often over forty miles an hour, are partners in creation, co-sculptors in hewing the chasms and creases that distribute the waters of West Maui. The rain flows down the sharp geology of Pu'u Kukui's slopes to create Honokōhau Stream, the longest in West Maui. On its journey seaward, at the head of Honokōhau Valley, a waterfall thunders to the valley floor some 1,700 feet below, in a cascade considered by some to be second in the country to California's Yosemite.[3] The waters sustain the surrounding conservation lands, more than 11,600 acres of green in one of the most biologically rich regions in the state. These lands represent one of Maui Land & Pineapple's most striking initiatives: a long-held commitment to protect West Maui's vital water source and the rare and endangered species of the region.

29

The precious jewel in this ecological crown is the Pu'u Kukui Watershed Preserve, at 8,304 acres the largest private preserve in Hawai'i. The PKW, as it is known, makes up the lion's share of Maui Land & Pineapple's conservation lands, sweeping from a 480-foot elevation to the summit and encompassing some of the last stands of pristine native rain forest in Hawai'i. Twelve of the 150 distinct plant communities in Hawai'i exist in this preserve, including nearly 350 known species of native Hawaiian plants.[4] Its ecosystems at various elevations include upland bogs of dwarfed vegetation, cloud and rain forests, and rare habitats for thousands of native insects and animals. *Makai*, toward the ocean, the PKW's coastal complement, the Makai Conservation Area (MCA), extends into the ocean with the Honolua-Mokulē'ia Marine Life Conservation District. The makai conservation lands include more than 3,600 acres and 11.5 miles of prime shoreline, stretching from Kapalua to Poelua bays. With their rare flora and fauna, the preserves are an environmental crucible governed by a forward-thinking ethic of stewardship. Even by the high standards of Hawai'i, the rugged West Maui Mountains are extraordinary in their biodiversity, a 52,000-acre habitat for known and yet-to-be discovered forms of life existing in their natural communities.[5]

Recognizing these treasures and the need to protect them, Colin Cameron, then-president of landowner ML&P, established the Pu'u Kukui Watershed Preserve in 1988. It was a conservation benchmark that spurred a fortuitous chain of events. In 1992, ML&P dedicated the preserve in perpetual easement to The Nature Conservancy of Hawai'i, and a year later it became one of the first private companies to join Hawai'i's landmark Natural Area Partnership Program. Its unique formula—for every dollar the company spends to protect the site, the state of Hawai'i contributes $2—was the first of its kind in the country, an unprecedented alliance between state government and a private landowner.

"There are plenty of examples of people donating land, but I can't think of another instance where the landowner has dedicated its land forever to conservation and then helped foot the bill to help pay for that conservation," Mark White, director of Maui programs for The Nature Conservancy of Hawai'i, told *National Wildlife* magazine in 1997.[6] In 1998, an additional layer of protection was formed when the preserve became part of the West Maui Mountain Watershed Partnership, an agreement between the state, county, and private landowners to protect the West Maui forest preserve.

The results of these initiatives are ubiquitous in the northwest Maui landscape. Green greets the eye in all directions, reflecting the preponderance of conservation and agriculture, the two most prevalent land uses in the area. Of the 23,000 acres in Kapalua Nui, more than half are in conservation, with the bulk of the remaining lands devoted to agriculture and open space. Planned development accounts for a very small percentage of the total land holdings. The stewards of the land recognize the vital role of nature in sustaining the communities of the future, and their priorities have not gone unrecognized. Under its Audubon Heritage Program, Audubon International has certified the company's comprehensive conservation program for its golf courses.

Kuleana, the Hawaiian word for interest and responsibility, describes the work of Randy Bartlett and his team, under whose care lie the protection, management, and stewardship of the conservation lands. Bartlett has been described as the *kahu 'āina*—the caretaker—of the preserve, and he is passionate about it.

"We see the last of Hawai'i's pristine native rainforests that even most *kama'āina*—those born and raised on Maui—don't get to experience in their lifetimes," he explained. "It is a rare privilege to do this work, to *mālama i ka 'āina*—care for the land. This work resonates very strongly with our own internal values as well as those of our employer. It may not make us rich in the material sense, but our lives are enriched and rewarded every moment we spend in the preserve, in ways that are priceless."

Next page: Hidden in Honokōhau Valley, a 1,700-foot waterfall is considered second in the country to California's Yosemite.

Of the 1,000 species of native flowering plants in Hawai'i, eighty-nine percent are endemic, growing nowhere else on the planet.[7] Bartlett's many years in and around the preserve have afforded him a macro- and micro-view of this world, from expansive panoramas of sacred places to the most infinitesimal botanical forms. One of those botanical jewels is the *liliwai (Acaena exigua)*, a tiny member of the rose family that was once common in the uplands of Maui and Kaua'i. Today it is a sad statistic, one of nine native plants in the preserve that are on the Endangered Species List of the U.S. Fish & Wildlife Service.

Liliwai was on the verge of being officially declared extinct in the spring of 1995. But in a remote area of Pu'u Kukui where they had been dropped off by helicopter, field technicians Hank Oppenheimer and Scott Meidell discovered a tiny plant the size of a half-dollar coin. To Bartlett, the last sighting of this plant—"the passing into possible extinction of what may have been the last liliwai plant ever seen in Hawai'i"—was one of the most poignant and remarkable events in the legacy of the preserve.

"Liliwai was once fairly common in the montane bogs of Maui and Kaua'i, but was last seen by PKW staff in December 1999," he recalled. "Although we've conducted several extensive surveys in the past six-plus years with help from the staff of the National Tropical Botanical Gardens on Kaua'i, we haven't discovered any since then.

"It's an incredibly sad feeling with a huge sense of loss—like losing a family member. After all, to Hawaiians, the plants of these islands were, and still are, recognized as *'ohana* (family) and are revered and respected as ancestral *kūpuna*, as elders."

Most people have never heard of liliwai, or of the other native plants in the PKW that are on the Endangered Species List. But to the environmental community and the stewards of the preserve, the names of the plants carry profound emotion and a sense of vigilance and longing: *māhoe (Alectryon macrococcus); pauoa* fern *(Ctenitis squamigera);*

31

haʻiwale (*Cyrtandra munroi*), a shrub in the African violet family, with only a hundred plants left in the wild; *Hesperomannia arborescens*, a small tree in the sunflower family, considered extinct on Lānaʻi; Lydgate's Pteris fern (*Pteris lidgatei*), believed to be extinct on Molokaʻi and found in only three valleys, including one in the PKW; *hāhā* (*Cyanea lobata and Cyanea magnicalyx*), a member of the lobelia family, called the "pride of Hawaiʻi's flora." On Lānaʻi, *hāhā* was last seen in 1934, and on Maui it had disappeared from the mid-1800s until it was rediscovered in 1982. Although those survivors died in a landslide a few years later, three plants were discovered on Puʻu Kukui in 1996, and five more nearby on state land.[8]

A flamboyant denizen of the preserve is *Lobelia gloria-montis*—"glory of the mountain," *puʻe* in Hawaiian, a dramatic endemic plant found only on Maui and neighboring Molokaʻi. Its large, pale yellow petals curl downward in a cluster on a stalk about two feet tall, conspicuous against the verdure of its upland habitat. Each plant flowers and blooms only once before dying. "This is one of the most spectacular flowering plants in the bogs," said Bartlett. "It only grows in these very special bog habitats of West Maui and Molokaʻi."

So dense is the peat in the bog soil that each foot of depth represents 10,000 years of accumulation and evolution.[9] A footprint could remain for decades. To protect this ecosystem and minimize the presence of humans, Bartlett and his staff have braved stinging winds and rain to build a miles-long boardwalk stretching from the summit to the trail head in the upper reaches of the preserve. Initially it took a decade to transport the materials and build the boardwalk in its remote location, but the pace of its construction, mile by arduous mile, has stepped up considerably in recent years.

"We've also had pigs all over the place, causing tremendous damage in the rainforest," he added. "They were bringing in the weeds and eating *hāpuʻu* tree ferns and creating mosquito breeding grounds

Preceding page: The treasures of the Puʻu Kukui Watershed Preserve include, *clockwise from top right,* the Hawaiian hydrangea; the lehua blossom; *Lobelia gloria-montis,* which grows only in special habitats of West Maui and Molokaʻi; and a young fern.

RANDY BARTLETT
Watershed Manager, Puʻu Kukui Watershed Preserve

Working in the Puʻu Kukui Watershed Preserve teaches me humility in the midst of the awe and wonder of creation. Whether you want to call that force Nature, or God, or anything else, as humans we have a spiritual, as well as practical, responsibility to care for and protect the other life forms that share this planet with us. Otherwise, we stand to lose much of what is beautiful and sacred.

I'm mindful and consciously aware of the fragility of nature. I therefore try to make the conscientious decisions and choices that I hope will lead my family and me down the path of a sustainable future—not just for us, but for mankind, because it all starts at home. This means that I constantly turn off the lights when I leave a room, compost our kitchen scraps, and collect piles of recycling materials in our garage, much to my wife's chagrin at times. But I think she's resigned to it after nearly a quarter-century of living with me!

In the Maunalei Arboretum, *'ōhi'a* trees sprout lehua blossoms, a favorite of the volcano goddess Pele.

that were spreading avian pox and malaria and killing the native birds." To stem this cycle of destruction, ML&P committed time and money to fencing off the area, and the results are impressive: most of the preserve has been free of pigs for longer than a decade.

The drippy habitat creates an infinite environment of green, but when the clouds part, even for an instant, the shoreline twinkles in the distance, adding silver and blue to the palette from this elevated vantage point. Violet Lake, a small, remote pond near the boardwalk, adds to the canvas. When the light is right, the cold waters of the mile-high pond appear violet with the reflection of the sky.

Its Hawaiian name, *Ki'owaiokiha*, recalls its origins as the mythic summit home of a water goddess, a *mo'o*, named *Kihawahine*. A personal family god of the great Maui chief Pi'ilani, Kihawahine is known as the *'aumakua* after whom he named his son, Kiha-a-Pi'ilani.[10]

Such legendary associations make this diminutive pond a sacred place in the *wao akua*, a realm of the gods. Hawaiian lore points to Ki'owaiokiha as the upland counterpart to Kihawahine's coastal dwelling, Mokuhinia pond at Moku'ula, the power point in Lahaina for Pi'ilani and generations of rulers who made Lahaina the capital of the kingdom.[11]

Of special interest to naturalists is Violet Lake's botanical namesake, *Viola maviensis*, the rare, tiny, endemic Maui violet, known for its fragrance and delicate beauty. The species also grows in one bog on Moloka'i and in bogs in the Kohala Mountains of Hawai'i Island. On Pu'u Kukui, they start blooming in early summer, said Bartlett, heralding the summit area's peak season for color. "The green swords will start blooming later in the summer," he continued. "The best time for flowers is late summer, especially at the top of the mountain. The lobelias and native

Next page: Tree canopies dapple the footpaths in the Maunalei Arboretum, where many rare species have been found.

gardenias in the area bloom in the late summer through September, and *koli'i* (*Trematolobelia macrostachys*), a native lobelia shrub, grows during late summer near the boardwalk."

The West Maui green swords and the West Maui 'Eke silversword (named after Mauna 'Eke) only grow in West Maui, Bartlett explained. "They're a different species from the silverswords on Haleakalā and in Ka'ū on the Big Island." Silversword Bog near the Pu'u Kukui summit is an otherworldly ecosystem of silvery, light green swords and the dwarfed plants typical of the acidic soil of the bogs. Trees such as *'ōhi'a* (*Metrosideros polymorpha*), common in the rainforests of Hawai'i, can reach 100 feet tall in other Hawaiian forests but in the bogs are dwarfed, like bonsai, to a mere four to six inches.[12]

Second in height to Pu'u Kukui, Mauna 'Eke, home of the 'Eke silversword, is a brooding caldera at the 4,480-foot elevation on the northern slope of Mauna Kahalawai. When the clouds around 'Eke part, those fortunate enough to get a glimpse see a flat-topped mountain with unique characteristics: a silhouette resembling a flat, dimpled loaf of bread, prompting the nickname "Bread Top Mountain" or "Bread Box Mountain."

Erosion of the soft cinders around 'Eke crater has left hard basalt with a network of surface pits. "These huge pits are like sinkholes through which the lava came up," Bartlett explained. "These lava tubes are vertical, and some of them are thirty, forty feet across and go straight down for hundreds of feet. It's not a place for just anybody to be walking around in. It's also a very rare bog environment, which makes it even more special. There are little ponds of water, shallow pools just a few inches deep. A very rare freshwater quillwort fern, *Isoetes hawaiiensi*, grows only on 'Eke and on the east slope of Mauna Kea on Hawai'i island." When seen from above during the silversword season, 'Eke crater is abundantly peppered with their silvery, sage-colored clusters.

"'Eke is not the summit of West Maui, but it is a sacred spot to Hawaiians," said Bartlett. "Our PKW boundary is on the edge of 'Eke, with Honokōhau Valley in back to the west of it. Our boundary skirts the western rim, and the summit of 'Eke is in the state's Kahakuloa Natural Area Reserve."

The Hawaiians of old also referred to the mountain as 'E'eke, after a man by that name who was turned to stone for committing adultery against his wife, Līhau. The vengeful goddess Pele turned Līhau into a mountain behind Olowalu and their son, Pu'ulaina, into a hill by that name to the northwest of Lahainaluna. In a saga of jealousy and pique, Pele then turned the beautiful Molokini, Pu'ulaina's wife, into the dramatic crescent-shaped islet today renowned for its snorkeling and dive sites in South Maui.[13]

From the uplands to the ocean, the landmarks of West Maui are habitats for countless forms of life, from honeycreepers and seabirds to one of the two native mammals of Hawai'i. Hawai'i's extreme geographic isolation—more than 2,000 miles from the nearest land mass—made it impossible for all but two mammals, the Hawaiian monk seal and the hoary bat, to travel,

Left: Mauna 'Eke cuts a curious silhouette at the edge of Honokōhau Valley and the Pu'u Kukui Watershed Preserve. *Above:* The 'Eke silversword in boggy Mauna 'Eke grows nowhere else in the world, not even in other parts of Maui.

unassisted, to the Islands over millions of years of evolution. The endemic form of the hoary bat, *'ōpe'ape'a*, (*Lasiuris cinereus semotus*), is the only native Hawaiian land mammal and one of two endangered native animals in the PKW. The other is the *'ua'u*, the Hawaiian dark-rumped petrel (*Pterodroma phaeopygia sandwichensis*) with a wingspan of up to thirty-six inches.

The Hawaiian petrels, which also favor Haleakalā Crater, nest from March to October under the *uluhe* ferns in the preserve. With their moaning calls and burrowed nests, these large, soot-colored seabirds are a sharp contrast to the delicate honeycreepers, the *'i'iwi*, *'apapane*, and *'amakihi*, that flit through the treetops as they gather nectar with their curved beaks. The endemic Hawaiian short-eared owl, *pueo* (*Asio*

flammeus sandwichensis), calls through the grasslands and forests with its muffled, bark-like hoots.

The *'a'o*, the Newell's shearwater (*Puffinus newelli*), a species listed "threatened," is heard but has yet to be seen. "We have heard them, so we know they're here," said Bartlett. "We haven't found any nests because they're usually on the steep cliffs that are hard to get to. They've just discovered a large colony on Lāna'i, and we have some of the same habitats."

Along the shoreline of Kapalua Resort, the calls of seabirds, some hauntingly human, can be heard at twilight as the adults forage for fish, squid, and crustaceans to feed their nesting chicks. At the summit and the ocean and the far reaches of the ahupua'a, precious water flows, sustaining myriad life forms along the way.

The Bays
OF PI'ILANI

Preceding pages: A blowhole at Nākālele Point marks the northernmost point of the island. *Left:* Hāwea Point features thriving reefs and unique coastal geology.

P i'ilani was a savvy ruler. His domain, the northwest coast of Maui, had fertile valleys, sandy beaches, cliffs, freshwater springs bubbling in the ocean, and a multitude of treasures from land and sea. He trusted his gods but kept a watchful eye for invaders, who nipped at the edges of Maui in search of food and land. From vantage points on the bluffs above the bays of northwest Maui, Pi'ilani's warriors scanned the channels and horizon for would-be usurpers who stealthily approached in their canoes.

"The populations on O'ahu and the smaller islands were much larger than their food sources could support," noted ninety-year-old Lahaina kama'āina Edna Pualani Farden Bekeart, who is researching the life of the six-teenth-century Maui chief. "Maui was a target because of its fertile valleys and abundant food plants. The lesser chiefs of O'ahu would board their canoes at dawn for northwest Maui, where they would try to steal plants and food. Pi'ilani set up his look-out points on the cliffs so he could watch for attackers from the ocean and send his fast canoes after them."

Nā Hono a Pi'ilani—the Bays of Pi'ilani—were sacred to Pi'ilani, said Bekeart. The lei of six bays was marked by a heiau at each end. "There was a heiau at the top of the black rock at Keka'a, Pu'u Keka'a, and another, Heakealani, at the northern end of the Bays, by Hononana near Kahakuloa.[1] These were sacred bays that were chosen by Pi'ilani from among many along the coast."

Bekeart's mission is to achieve federal recognition for Lower Honoapi'ilani Road as a Heritage Corridor acknowledging Pi'ilani and the six historic bays named after him. Lower Honoapi'ilani Road reaches three of the six bays, and access to the remaining bays is through land owned by ML&P, the state, and private landowners.

Unlike its better-known mauka counterpart, Honoapi'ilani Highway, the road skirts the northwest coastline from Honokōwai, the first of the bays, to shortly past Kapalua Beach, formerly named Fleming Beach. With its cliffs, bays, coves, and curvy shoreline of sandy beaches and thriving coral gardens, this section of the northwest Maui coastline was appreciated for its cultural and spiritual significance long before it became known as a modern recreational nexus.

A 3.5-mile coastal trail will take shoreline access up a notch by linking five of Maui's top beaches in the area. The proximity of Lāna'i and Moloka'i across two channels, Pailolo and 'Au'au, gives the new pedestrian pathway the same unparalleled view as Pi'ilani's six-teenth-century vantage points. The Kapalua Coastal Trail is part of the ongoing renaissance of Kapalua, the master-planned resort revolving around three of the company's ten contiguous ahupua'a in West Maui.

The trail is a modern application of the ancient ahupua'a system in which communities were connected by a network of coastal and mauka-to-makai trails. Stretching from Lower Honoapi'ilani Road to Honolua Bay, the Kapalua Coastal Trail is part of a larger, 100-mile network of trails planned throughout the resort.

Eleven-and-a-half miles of prime shoreline along this coast make up ML&P's makai conservation lands, an essential component of the company's environmental initiatives. The makai conservation lands include the Honolua-Mokulē'ia Marine Life Conservation District, established by the State Board of Land and Natural Resources in 1978.[2] By prohibiting fishing and the taking of marine life within the conservation area, the conservation designation boosts the entire marine food chain. Brilliant fish and rich, thriving coral reefs saturate the bays with life and color, luring wide-eyed spectators to its vivid underwater gardens.

It was along this coastline, at Honolua Bay, that one of Polynesia's most powerful cultural endeavors was launched. The Polynesian Voyaging Society chose Honolua Bay as the departure site for the first trans-Pacific voyage of *Hōkūleʻa*, the sixty-foot double-hulled canoe that made a historic journey to Tahiti in 1976. It was the first of many long-distance voyages *Hōkūleʻa* has completed without the use of modern navigational instruments.

While Honolua was selected for the particular wind patterns of the Pailolo Channel, its scenic beauty and underwater vitality are the features that attract beachgoers. "Honolua has the best snorkeling on the island," offered Kihapiʻilani William Kinney Kaina, who can trace his genealogy to the chief Piʻilani, and whose grandparents, Bernard and Orpha Kaina, were longtime employees of ML&P's Honolua Plantation. "There's a boundary line from point to point across the bay; inside of that line, you can't fish, dive, or lay a net. The fish grow to be huge, and there are many schools of *āholehole*." Kaina, thirty, is an accomplished waterman, a free diver certified as a lifeguard, who has an intimate knowledge of this coastline.

"Honolua on a good day is regarded by many surfers as the best surf break on Maui and one of the best surfing spots in the world," raved surfer and author John R. K. Clark in *The Beaches of Maui County*, his classic and authoritative beach guide. "On a big winter day the cliffs above the bay are lined with surfers and spectators watching the often crowded action in the surf below." In an interview in 2007, Clark added, "Ask a hundred surfers where the perfect wave is, and many of them will say, 'Honolua.'"[3] Perhaps that is why the first surfing contest at the bay was organized by Dick Brewer, a renowned surfer and surfboard manufacturer.

As a young boy growing up in the area, Kiha Kaina developed keen oceanic instincts and a love for Kapalua Beach, designated "America's Best Beach" in 2006 by "Dr. Beach" Stephen Leatherman, professor and director of the Laboratory for Coastal Research at Florida International University. Old-timers know it as Fleming Beach, named after David T. Fleming, the avid horticulturalist and manager, from 1912, of ML&P's predecessors, Honolua Ranch and Baldwin Packers. When Kapalua Resort opened in the mid-1970s, the old Fleming Beach was renamed Kapalua Beach, and the beach at Honokahua Bay became D. T. Fleming Beach Park.

The reefs in the Honolua-Mokulēʻia Marine Life Conservation District provide ideal conditions for snorkeling.

ORPHA KAINA

Former resident of Honolua Plantation

When my grandson was about eight or nine years old, my husband felt a need to teach him everything he knew about the ocean. And Honolua Bay was where he took his two grandsons. Lono was young, so he stayed with me and watched. Kiha went with his grandfather. They started from the middle part of the right hand side of the bay, where the surfers go down to go surfing. And they went from shore all the way out into the deep ocean, slowly. We watched them from the top.

It was such a beautiful sight to see Grandpa in the ocean with his grandson. Kiha stayed close to Grandpa's side. They had their own goggles and fins, and they swam. Grandpa showed him what the crevices looked like, showed him the different kinds of fishes, what grew on the reef, the colors, what it looked like from above the water looking down, compared to when you're in the water. He showed him the camouflage of the squid, the rich reefs, what kinds of fish live in the reefs. Then he took Kiha to the center part of the bay, the coral gardens. He showed him what to expect when they left the gardens: the deep, deep ocean, where you cannot see the bottom, and how

the waves slide with the wind. He showed him the direction of the wind and how the waves follow, and the different types of currents. Then he took him out further, way out, deeper. He showed him the bigger fishes, the bigger *honu* (turtles).

He took him a little to the right of the bay to feel the kind of current that was there, where Līpoa Point is. He showed him how the water can change, and how sometimes, when you're on the shore and you look at the water, the water looks nice, but when you start diving or fishing, the water changes. It's because of the direction of the wind.

The boy learned all of that on that day. Today, that boy is certified to be a lifeguard. He was certified to be a junior lifeguard at thirteen. Now all he needs to know is how to sew his own net. Lono could be a lifeguard too.

My husband didn't know that he wouldn't live much longer. He just said, 'Before anything happens to me, I want my grandsons to know how to fish, how to dive, how to swim, and the different strokes to use.' That's what Grandpa showed them that day, and that's why that bay is so special to me.

The lava "teeth" of Makāluapuna
Point are a distinctive feature of
the coastline.

"Kapalua was my favorite spot when I was younger because it had the most fish and it's the prettiest bay by far, with public access," said Kaina. "It's the most protected of all the bays in the area, and there's a nice surf spot outside called Scorpion Bowl that only the locals know about. It has some of the scariest waves in the world. The coral there is sharp and stings you, and the waves break right on the rocks." Kaina noted that he caught his first fish at Kapalua Bay, not far from where he saw his first octopus, a five-pound creature skillfully camouflaged in color and habitat.

The gentle beach is a perfect white-sand crescent, bordered at north and south ends by rocky points that embrace the bay along a shoreline of picture-perfect coconut trees. Kapalua means "two borders," and the beach, protected by an offshore coral reef, is one of West Maui's most popular swimming and snorkeling spots.

Local residents like Kaina and his family still refer to the beaches by their nicknames: "Fleming's" for Kapalua Beach, "Slaughterhouse" for Mokulē'ia, "Windmills" for Punalau (officially named Keonehelele'i Beach, meaning "scattered sand"), "Stables" for D. T. Fleming Beach Park at Honokahua. With their roots in ranching and plantation life, the names hark back to pre-resort times when the community was centered around Honolua Ranch and the plantation.

"I still refer to Kapalua Beach as 'Fleming's,'" commented Wayne Carroll, former irrigation supervisor who retired from ML&P after forty-two years. "And if you tell the old-timers, 'Go to Stables,' they'll go straight to D. T. Fleming, because that's where they kept the horses for the *paniolo* (cowboys) during the old ranch days. Punalau is called 'Windmills' because there was a windmill there, near a corral. The corral was where they used to bed down the cattle, and the windmill

was used to draw water from the springs to water down the horses and cattle. Over at Punalau, there were so many springs that if you go into the water at the shore, you can feel the icy brackish water from the springs."

In the drier areas of Hawai'i, the Hawaiians of old had the ingenuity to harvest drinking water from freshwater springs that bubbled into the ocean. The gatherer would enter the ocean with an empty vessel, an *ipu* (gourd), stoppered by a finger. The mouth of the ipu would be placed on the spring, which filled the vessel with water that could then be carried home. In the earlier, more innocent plantation era, when fewer demands were made on the environment, Carroll, an irrigation expert, was able to find fresh water at the shoreline through his own keen instincts.

"When I'd go to the beach to dive or throw a net, and my kids were thirsty, I knew where I could make a hole in the sand about a foot and a half deep, and fresh water would appear," he recalled. "We'd use goggles to scoop it up. We could wash ourselves with it and even drink it. It didn't taste salty. It just tasted like regular, clean river water—cool, like it had run down from the mountain." Carroll and other kama'āina have fond recollections of camping at the seashore in times past and using fresh water from the springs to cook rice on the campfire.

The marine life and natural resources exist in a delicate, integrated ecosystem that requires vigilance and care. The modern stewards of these lands still apply the timeless principles of the indigenous Hawaiians, who were supremely skilled in aquaculture long before the word became known. They maintained their fishing grounds with sensible rules to prevent depletion of their important coastal resources. Fishing was *kapu*, taboo, during spawning periods, and no one took more from the ocean than what was needed.

"From growing up here, I learned to study the fish and to know when they've come in to lay eggs," explained Carroll. "Every fish is different, and they all have their reproductive cycles and time periods. As great fishermen, the Hawaiians knew this."

Orpha Kaina, Kiha Kaina's grandmother, remembered the quiet wisdom of her late husband, Bernard, who was known as a consummate waterman. "When we came to the shore, we could never be upset or loud," she explained. "He'd say, 'Sit quietly. The fish have eyes.' That means the fish can see you. To a fisherman, the ocean is not a place to play or talk loudly. There are principles to follow, such as, 'When you come out of the water, you always share the fish.'"

Once, she recounted, he caught six *moi*, the delicate threadfish so precious that it was reserved for royalty in pre-contact times, and violators were subject to the death penalty. "Moi is my favorite fish, but he didn't tell me he caught them until two days later," she recalled. "I asked, 'Where's the moi?' And he told me, 'There were people on the shore, so I gave them away.' He was very thoughtful, very kind."

That practice also applied to the home, she said. "No one would ever leave a Hawaiian home without something in their hands: *'opihi*, banana, fish. That's how people lived in the ahupua'a. They gave with their hearts. They knew that when you share, more will come."

"I never knew there were so many practices," added her grandson, Kiha. "I learned that when you go to the beach, you shouldn't leave the house on bad terms. Always leave in good spirits, and don't go if you have argued, or if there's trouble at home. Every time we catch fish, we always split the catch evenly with the families that came with us. The rule of the ocean is always to share and never to be greedy. My grandpa taught us to never turn our backs to the water, even if it's crystal clear and flat. The older Hawaiians take their superstitions seriously. They believe in all this, and I respect it too."

For many generations, families like the Kainas and Carrolls have fished and gathered *limu*, the often edible multicolored seaweeds that thrive along the shoreline. "If we want green limu, we know where to go," said Wayne Carroll, a lifelong fisherman and diver. "*Limu-kohu* (a succulent red seaweed), we only gather during *Kona* (leeward) winds, because it grows on rocks and is difficult to pick during trade winds. When there are

Kona winds, the limu-kohu is bountiful. We clip it or pull very lightly, leaving the roots so the plant can continue growing. We were taught to just pick what we need, and to leave the plant for the future."

Carroll favors limu *pepe'e*, a fern-like sea vegetable, which grows in the tidal pools and is difficult to discern in the water. "My wife, Pearl, taught our children to wait until the sun is directly above and lights up the tidal pool. She taught them to look for the golden glow—that is the limu—and only then to pick it. When you can't see the gold, you never reach in, because there may be a *puhi* (eel) hiding there." Carroll said they'd mix the limu with *'opihi* (limpets), *wana* (sea urchin), and filets of *kūmū* (goatfish) that they had gathered and prepared. "*'Ono* (delicious) is the only way to describe it!"

Reading the weather and wind patterns has always been an arcane art form for residents of the region. A trademark of northwest Maui, the idiosyncrasies of the wind are caused by the proximity of Lāna'i and Moloka'i across the channels. "When it's clear and unusually calm, and Moloka'i looks like it's moved closer to Maui, a storm is coming, you can almost be assured of that," explained Carroll. "When it's calm and you can't feel any wind, there's a storm system out there that is blocking it, coming from north to south."

The wind currents sweep over the plantation and down to Honokōwai. Avoiding Kā'anapali, he explained, the wind swoops out into the channel between Lāna'i and Moloka'i, from the Pailolo to the 'Au'au Channel. "If you look at our history, when we have rain and trade winds here, they will not reach Lahaina. But if it's the Kona wind coming toward us from the south, everything gets wet, and nothing is exceptional. The Hawaiians took advantage of that. They could read the winds and prepare for them."

The shoreline vegetation in northwest Maui also must be tolerant of the elements. Many of the coastal plants are culturally significant, with multiple uses in crafts and village life. The handsome, hardy *hala* (*Pandanus tectorius*) has pineapple-like fruit and

Preceding page: At rocky Hāwea Point, unusual formations appear unpredictably.

thorny, spiky leaves that rustle in the wind like coconut fronds. A Hawaiian cultural staple, hala has leaves that are woven into *lauhala* mats, baskets, sails, and accessories. It was shared with the upland dwellers of old, and its fibrous hala fruit was eaten in times of famine. When dried, the bristled, hair-like fruit tips were used as brushes for the native dyes, to adorn the *kapa* they made of pounded *wauke* bark. One of the materials used to scent the precious kapa was the fragrant *'iliahialo'e* (*Santallum ellipticum*), the endemic coast sandalwood that grows in the region with cream-colored blossoms and olive-like fruit.

The indigenous *milo* (*Thespesia populnea*), with its heart-shaped leaves and hibiscus-like yellow blossoms, also grows well in the saline soil and provides shade and beauty along the shore. Its wood is prized in calabashes and canoe building, its bark was used for cordage, and its leaves, seeds, and flowers were useful in *hana aloha*, the ancient practice of love magic. *"He milo ka lā'au, mimilo ke aloha,"* goes the saying: "Milo is the plant; love goes round and round."[4]

The shrubby *'ūlei* (*Osteomeles anthyllidifolia*) with its dainty white flowers, used in lei, may be common in coastal areas, but there is nothing common about its branches, willowy enough to be made into scoop nets for shrimp and fish. In contrast to its rose-like flowers, its strong wood was used to make digging sticks and fish spears.[5] The endemic

'āwiwi (*Centaurium sebaeoides*) is endangered and rarely seen, but when it appears, with its white or pale pink flowers and pointed, fleshy leaves, it will likely be after a rainy winter spell.

Unlike 'āwiwi, the common and abundant *naupaka* (*Scaevola taccada*) is prevalent along the coast, and useful, too. When its succulent leaf is squeezed and its moisture applied to a snorkeling mask, it becomes an instant and effective de-fogger. Its delicate white flower appears to be incomplete, evoking the Hawaiian legend of two star-crossed lovers who were torn apart by class differences. The half-flower of lowland naupaka and its mauka counterpart, the mountain naupaka, are said to represent the two lovers.

Pele's gentle sister, Hi'iaka-i-ka-poli-o-Pele, also has a presence at this shoreline. Her namesake, the *pā'ū-o-Hi'iaka* (*Jacquemontia ovalifolia sandwicensis*), is a native morning glory with fragile blue petals and petite, rounded leaves. The name means "skirt of Hi'iaka" and refers to Pele's day at the beach with her baby sister. After leaving her sister on the beach and upon returning from a fishing trip, Pele found that the vines of this plant had grown over Hi'iaka to cool and protect her from sunburn.[6] As an adult, Hi'iaka is said to have stopped in Kahakuloa, just north of Honokōhau, on her mythical journey to Moloka'i with her best friend, Hōpoe. She rested near the sea cliff and is said to have left her spirit in a boulder there.[7]

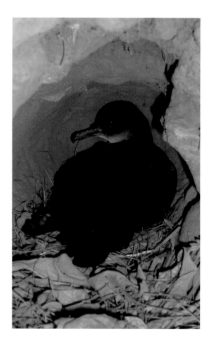

Like Hiʻiaka, a fleet of annual avian visitors makes purposeful journeys across the Pailolo Channel. Every year from March until November, the wedge-tailed shearwaters, ʻuaʻu kani, animate the skies with their aerobatic forms above a rocky point north of Kapalua Beach. Their nesting season is welcomed by conservationists, who tagged 220 fledglings at the colony in 2007, an increase of 93 over the previous year. It is the largest known ʻuaʻu kani colony in Maui Nui. More than 200,000 pairs of these seabirds are estimated to live in the Northwestern Hawaiian Islands, with 40,000 to 60,000 more in the main Hawaiian Islands.[8] The monogamous avian creatures return to the same site every year to lay one egg per nest, in natural crevices, ironwood roots, or in burrows they have dug in the sandy soil with their bills and feet.

The birds have thirty-eight-inch wing spans and emit moans, groans, and wails that sound hauntingly like humans. They are cryptic creatures that arrive at dusk, leave before sunrise, and spend much of the day in unseen realms at sea. They feed their young with regurgitated seafood and are paradoxically resilient and fragile, migrating long distances over open ocean yet easily disoriented by artificial lights on land. When these grayish-brown seabirds soar at dusk and dawn, they lend otherworldly dimensions to the area.

The earthbound nests are in a site along the 11.5-mile coastal trail under development by ML&P. Vulnerable to cats, dogs, and rodents, the colony was regenerated by the efforts of seventy-five-year-old Isao Nakagawa, a retiree of ML&P who is lauded for his conservation initiative. "At one time, I counted something like twenty-two dead birds there," he recalled. "I thought something had to be done." He approached a couple who had access to the area, Craig and Maja Ramsey, who granted him access to the site and purchased cat traps which Nakagawa then vigilantly managed.[9]

"They were really good in helping," said Nakagawa. "I started baiting the traps, and I was catching mongooses, cats, and rats—big rats, huge ones." He encouraged the couple to install a water line to re-vegetate the area. Boulders were rearranged to block loiterers and vehicular traffic. Working with wildlife biologist Fern Duvall of the Department of Land and Natural Resources, Nakagawa was the driving force that ignited wider efforts to preserve the colony.

"He was down on his hands and knees and he'd grab the birds and they'd bite him," Duvall told the *Honolulu Advertiser* on March 14, 2007, referring to the bird tagging of 2006. "His hands were bloody, but he was so happy."

When the shearwaters' nesting season ends for the year, new migrants appear on the horizon. Humpback whales, their massive gray mounds glowing silver in the sunlight, frolic, mate, and calve in the channels during their annual winter migration. Fleeing to summery Hawai'i from the icy waters of Alaska, the whales transform beach-going into a spectator sport. Surfers look up from their boards, children point from the shore, and enthusiastic rubberneckers squint at the horizon through binoculars. Five hundred years ago, Pi'ilani's sentinels watched for marauders from their cliffside vantage points. Today the eyes are welcoming, searching for surfers, whales, and birds.

At Honolua Bay in 1976, *Hōkūle'a* stocked up on provisions for its maiden voyage to Tahiti.

SAM KA'AI

Silla Kaina, who grew up in Honolua Plantation, remembered the day her father drove their family to the sea cliffs to watch history being made. It was May 1, 1976, and the Polynesian voyaging canoe, *Hōkūle'a*, "Star of Gladness," was about to depart on its maiden voyage from Honolua Bay to Tahiti. After years of preparation, the sixty-foot double-hulled canoe was poised to prove that the ancient Polynesians could cross thousands of miles of open ocean without instruments, using only the wind, stars, clouds, and waves as their navigational guides. The voyage of *Hōkūle'a* was big national news—the National Geographic Society was there to document it—and Honolua was the chosen bay: the last point of land the voyagers would touch before reaching Tahiti. The sea cliffs that day gave the Kainas a vantage point on the ceremony; the bay and beach were *kapu*, off limits to the public, while the crew members assembled their provisions for their 3,000-mile transPacific voyage.

"It was so beautiful," recalled Kaina, who was ten years old at the time. "You could see the mascot, Maxwell the pig, and the chicken, and we heard Sam Ka'ai blow his conch shell here and there. That was the first time I heard the different sounds of the conch being blown." Maxwell, the chicken, and Hōkū, a dog, were taken along as proof that animals could also make the voyage.

Kaina recalled that it was *pau hana* time. The sun was getting low and her father was finished with work. "He put all of us in his Jeep," she remembered. "We asked him why he wanted to see *Hōkūle'a*, and he said it intrigued him to see all these people putting things on the canoe, making sure that the ropes and cordage were good."

Honolua Bay was chosen for the launch because of its unique wind patterns. "Why Honolua?" pondered Herb Kawainui Kāne, a founder of the Polynesian Voyaging Society and the designer and builder of the double-hulled canoe. "We felt that, from Honolua Bay and up around the north side of the island, we could pick winds that would carry the canoe away from land—clean, clear air without a lot of disruptions caused by the presence of land. Good, straight trade winds: sailing air. The cove from which *Hōkūle'a* departed offered protection from winds and surf, and after clearing the point, the canoe caught the Northeast Tradewinds and was on its way."

Cultural practitioner and master carver Sam Ka'ai, assisted by Honokōhau taro farmers Aimoku and Lehua Pali, spent days clearing the area and gathering and preparing food. "We gathered coconut, cooking banana, sweet potato, *'ulu* (breadfruit), and *kalo* (taro)," Ka'ai recalled. "We had all protocol foods. The *imu* (underground oven) was at Honolua Bay."

Each food has a deeper meaning in Hawaiian culture, said Ka'ai, and certain foods, such as *'ōpae* (shrimp) and *he'e* (squid or octopus), were not appropriate. "'Ōpae is a backward-swimming, small-minded, fuzzy-headed creature," explained Ka'ai, "and he'e is slippery. One of the meanings for he'e is to flee with abandonment, so you don't have he'e at a ceremony like this."

Limu kala, a long brown seaweed, is also used in ceremonies, and only one leaf is eaten. "It has needles; it's sharp," said Ka'ai. "You chew only one leaf as a symbol of letting this difficult trial pass, and to begin and finish well. 'Ulu is eaten so your endeavor bears fruit. Finally, you finish with making your mouth sweet. You eat *mai'a momona* (sweet banana). Eating the banana sweetens the satisfaction."

Mau Piailug, the Micronesian navigator who taught celestial navigation to the crew, stayed with Ka'ai at his home in Honokōhau Valley. "When I climbed the coconut tree, Mau thought I was climbing too slowly and told me to come down," said Ka'ai. "He put a rope around his leg, climbed up a thick

haole koa tree, then shifted over to the coconut tree and picked, he was that agile. We grated coconut by hand and boiled it to make milk, then pounded taro that we cooked. That taro, no can touch the hands. It lasts long that way. We heaped it up with a spatula, dipped it in coconut milk, and wrapped it in steamed banana leaves. We put thirty-nine pieces on the canoe. It was spirit food for Mau. He ate it once a day." Sea rations for the voyage included sweet potatoes, dried fish, and dried bananas, augmented by fresh fruit and vegetables from Maui.

Ka'ai had ordered *lauhala* (woven pandanus) mats four feet wide by forty feet long. He spread them on the ground at Honolua Bay and conducted a traditional 'awa ceremony for about thirty people, using a ceremonial eight-legged bowl to serve a drink made of freshly pounded 'awa root.

In the ceremony, as reported in the *Honolulu Advertiser*, Ka'ai told the gathering, "I do not know what frailties you take with you, but the sea will wash them out of you. The sea will give you mana and you will come back as new men."[1] Thirty years later, Ka'ai reflected, "I told them, 'You need to pray. People are going to risk their lives.' It started to rain, the water roared."

Ka'ai had carved two *ki'i*, a male statue and a female statue with mother-of-pearl eyes. "I chose one person to hold the female and one person to hold the male," he explained. "I told the crew: 'When you hear the shell blow on *Hōkūle'a*, your voyage will have begun. From this time, there will be no contact with the people of the land.'"

As Silla Kaina, her family, and other spectators watched from the cliffs, Ka'ai was paddled out to the canoe on the flat waters of the bay. He climbed aboard and lashed the ki'i to the *manu*, the stern pieces. With the blowing of the shell, the *kani ka pū*, the spiritual voyage had begun, and the sound rang out in all directions.

Thirty-three days and 2,800 miles later, *Hōkūle'a* sailed into a lagoon in Papeete to a welcoming crowd of 25,000 Tahitians on a day that was declared a national holiday.[2] Since then, *Hōkūle'a* has sailed more than 100,000 miles to all corners of the Polynesian Triangle and has enriched the lives of tens of thousands of people. In language, music, dance, education, navigation, and the Hawaiians' quest for self-knowledge, the voyage that was launched at Honolua Bay that day has only accelerated with time.

Left: Sam Ka'ai and the male and female *ki'i* he carved and lashed to *Hōkūle'a*.

The Land
OF PLENTY

Preceding pages: D. T. Fleming
planted Kapalua's Cook pines in
the early 1900s. *Left:* Honolua Store
is considered the heart of the resort.

Wes Nohara drives regularly along a narrow, winding road shaded by stately rows of Cook pines planted nearly one hundred years ago. When he was an infant in nearby Honolua Village, those pines were nearly half a century old. Now they have doubled in age, and Nohara is no longer the quiet youth who played marbles, climbed mango trees, and worked summers in the pineapple fields to pay for his college education. He is the third generation in his family to have lived and worked in Honolua, and while his pineapple-picking days are behind him, he is still immersed in agriculture as the general manager of Kapalua Farms.

"Everyone worked in the fields," he remembered. "It was a way of life, a lifestyle that everyone accepted." Nohara pointed mauka from where he sat on the plantation-style veranda of the Kukui Room on Office Road. "That little red roof, that's the old cannery," he said. "It was built in 1914. Things look different now than they did then. Some houses burned down, some houses were built. There was a theater, but if you go back far enough to the era of silent movies, there was a silent movie theater, too. And we had gardens. Everyone grew their own vegetables to supplement their modest income from agriculture."

A stone's throw from Nohara, the red-and-white Honolua Store, built in 1929, bustled with lunchtime patrons greeting friends, lining up at the deli, or noshing on the veranda before golf or a tennis match. The plantation-style building showed little change since it opened its doors decades ago. Across from the store's parking lot, in a similarly styled building, resort guests

from around the world checked in at what was once the headquarters of the plantation. The building was the plantation's lifeline, the dispensary and village post office from which residents of the nearby camps communicated with the rest of the world for nearly forty years.

Plantation life revolved around agriculture, the staple of northwest Maui. In a beautiful and bountiful environment, generations of workers lived a hard-scrabble life in the fields and valleys of Honolua Plantation, the predecessor of Kapalua Resort. Although good weather, fertile soil, and plentiful water from Pu'u Kukui were the legacy of the land, it took sweat and sacrifice to build a plantation that would become the economic and social foundation of the community. Ranching and the first glimmerings of commercial agriculture held out their promise in the 1800s. To the native plantings of taro and sweet potato were added a cattle ranch and a coffee farm, followed by diversified crops: aloe, watermelon, mango, avocado, mangosteen, star fruit, litchi, corn, macadamia nuts, rambutan—and, finally, pineapple. Many of the crops were short-term experiments, but the spiky-crowned *halakahiki* took root and stayed. Fearless vision and an industrious community helped make pineapple an economic mainstay of northwest Maui.

Henry Perrine Baldwin, an East Maui sugar planter, originally planned a sugar plantation when he ventured west in the late 1880s. His brother, D. Dwight Baldwin, had planted pineapple in East Maui's Ha'ikū. Together they established the pineapple industry on Maui with their Haiku Fruit and Packing Company. When H. P.

55

Baldwin rode his horse from Haʻikū to West Maui to revisit his Lahaina roots, he stopped in Honolua Valley and introduced a world of new prospects to the region. He visited a coffee farm managed by Richard C. Searle, a friend of Queen Liliʻuokalani. So taken was he by the operation that he established Honolua Ranch and plantation and hired David T. Fleming to take over upon Searle's retirement in 1911.

H. P. Baldwin died that year, but Fleming proved more than worthy of tackling the challenges ahead. A devoted forester, he immediately ordered seedlings and embarked on a vigorous tree-planting campaign. He planted trees to prevent erosion, conserve water, and block the sometimes fierce winds of the region. "The ranch received two truckloads of Eucalyptus Resinifera from the nursery of the Maui Agricultural Company," reads a handwritten entry from the company's forestry journal of December 1914.[1] "700 were planted on the windward boundary of Honokohau and the rest will be planted around Honokahua near the laborers' quarters." From March 1917: "4,000 Rostrata were planted along gulch sides near the camps and about the same number along roads. Ironwoods are preferable for the latter, but the stock eat it." From November 1917: "The Eucalyptus Rostrata seedlings arrived and there are now 20,000 trees ready to be planted." From January 1919: "50,000 trees have been planted." Of the hundreds of thousands of eucalyptus, cedar, teak, mahogany, ironwoods, junipers, Sugi pines, and other species planted throughout the ahupuaʻa, the regal rows of Cook and Norfolk pines remain the signature of Kapalua Resort.

The development of infrastructure and a flurry of planting—trees, pineapples, experimental fruit—marked Fleming's forty-year tenure with the company. He was also a postmaster for thirty-six of those years, a staggering revelation considering the sheer multitude of his activities. Soon after he started with the company on New Year's Day, 1912, the first twenty acres of pineapple were planted. That same year, construction began on the Honolua Ditch system to replace the

antiquated wooden flumes of the 1902 Honokōhau Ditch.[2] Honolua Ranch workers wielded picks and shovels on mountain precipices and blasted seventy tons of dynamite through lava. Eighteen months after construction began, water rushed down the mountain to the lowlands in the new Honolua Ditch. Of the 7 miles in the system, nearly 6.5 miles were tunnels, and the absence of fatalities was considered a miracle.[3] Today the Honolua Ditch system distributes water throughout Kapalua Resort, the Honolua pineapple lands, and areas in the Maui County water system.

Wayne Carroll, a retired irrigation supervisor for ML&P, was humbled by the skills he witnessed in his forty-two years with the company. Some of the old-timers passed on their knowledge before they retired. "Even

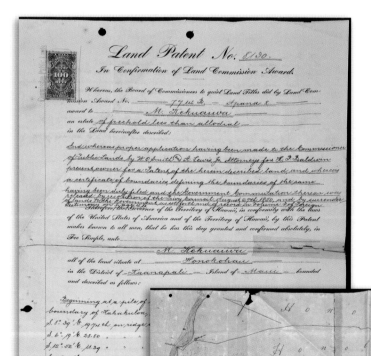

Above: Stone loʻi markers were used to number the taro fields, which at one time numbered 1,133 in Honokōhau Valley alone. *Below*: The expansive lands of Kapalua Resort are made up of ahupuaʻa that are intact, acquired in a series of land transactions, as shown in these documents, beginning in the 1880s.

WES NOHARA

General Manager, Kapalua Farms and Maui Pineapple Company

Our pineapple business evolved considerably through the years. There was a time in our history when we were farming with horses and animals, and then we went to trains and trucks, gas engines, diesel engines, and tractors. A railcar—a train—took the finished product out of the cannery in the village to the port in Lahaina to be shipped off.

Things changed in the village too. The Kumulani Chapel sits right over what used to be the asphalt of the old basketball court. Our football field was a triangular piece of grass. We used to make our own games, and there were seasons, like marble season, beanbag season, and home run season, when we played a game called home run. There was a game called steal-the-goal. We made our own sports or recreation: climbing trees, picking green mangoes, going to the gulch and eating guava, picking macadamia nuts. We even chased cows for the heck of it. The beach was a major part of our lives, so we went to the beach a lot to swim, play king-of-the-island, and surf. Some of the guys used sand boards.

At the Scout Hall Quonset hut and the old theater, they'd have giant parties and invite the whole village, so everyone was there, whether they were Filipino, Hawaiian, or Japanese, whether it was a wedding or a birthday.

in our ditches, numbers were carved into the walls," he explained. "When you look at what they did, especially at that time, you can't help but marvel at what they accomplished. They were skilled masons who could read the grain in the rock. Just by 'reading' the grain of the rock, they knew how to cut it."

Some of the plantation workers had specialized skills in masonry from making gravestones in their homeland of Japan. "We were working on a rock wall," recalled Carroll. "We were trying to crack these large rocks with sledgehammers. Nothing was breaking, and sparks were flying around. I remember Mr. Yabui, whose father was a master rock carver. He stopped me and said, 'Can you see the grain?' I said, 'I can't see anything.' He took his little hammer and just went ting-ting-ting, and the rock split open perfectly. He said to me, 'You'll learn.'"

Masons also carved numbers into large, smooth rocks that marked the *lo'i*—the taro fields—up and down the ahupua'a, in the valleys and on the slopes. Maps and records in the ML&P archive report that these lo'i numbered at least 1,133 in Honokōhau Valley at one time, in the days before taro was replaced by more easily cultivated crops. In the heyday of taro

farming, recalled the late Shigeto Nishimura, four mule wagons hauled taro twice a week to Lahaina.[4]

Soon after Fleming's arrival in 1912, construction on a cannery began on what is now Office Road. With its coffee mill and administration buildings, Honolua Ranch headquarters moved to higher ground, to the ahupua'a named Honokahua. Despite this change of location to a different ahupua'a, the village retained its original moniker. The move signaled the birth of a cohesive community as facilities were consolidated and plantation camps sprouted throughout Honokahua. Two years after the relocation, the new Office Road cannery opened, and a hydroelectric plant in Honokahua, also known as the "Powerhouse," sent its first currents of light and power through the village.

The hardships of creating and modernizing infrastructure are virtually invisible in the blur of twenty-first-century technology and contemporary notions of convenience. Faucets and switches are turned, and water and light miraculously appear. The rigors of plantation life, physically demanding and economically austere, are largely forgotten by all but those who lived through them, many of whom are now elderly or deceased.

The canning labels of ML&P's predecessors—Honolua Ranch, Baldwin Packers, and Alexander & Baldwin's Maui Pineapple Company—are a form of vintage art as well as a historic record.

Workers arose before dawn for prickly work in the cannery and back-breaking labor in the fields. Henrietta Mahuna, her memory keen at eighty-seven years old, worked twenty-two years in the hot sun and was the first woman supervisor in the Honolua pineapple fields. She moved to Honolua from Kaupō, East Maui, in 1942. "When I first started in the fields, I earned 20 cents an hour," she recalled. "When the union came, I got 45 cents an hour, and my husband was earning $1.20 an hour at the ranch. It went up to $1.45 an hour, and then $1.90." Her husband, Solomon Mahuna, was a respected *paniolo*, a fabled bronco buster who could ride, rope, shoe horses, and brand cattle. In the booklet *Plantation Days*, Robert Ohigashi told ML&P interviewers that despite earning just $1.75 a day as a student pineapple picker, he was still able to buy an encyclopedia with one summer's earnings and pay for his first semester's tuition at St. Anthony School. It wasn't just field work that was challenging. John Harrison Foss Jr., whose father supervised the construction of the Honolua Ditch, described what he saw on a visit to the cannery: women using chopsticks to handle the pineapple. It was impossible to use bare hands, he said, because the acid was "beyond belief."[5]

In their new location in Honokahua, with residential camps sprouting around them, the post office and store grew in importance. Mail arrived only twice a week for many years, and the postman made deliveries on horseback, traveling to and from Lahaina. The system, though slow, was profitable. "The post office serviced about 600 people from the camps and surrounding area," wrote Sylvia Hunt, retired ML&P historian, in the *Kapalua Nature Journal*.[6] "It made about $35,000 a month, a goodly sum in those days." Rural delivery began in 1957, decades after the cannery in Honokahua closed and the operations had shifted to Lahaina.

The growth of the community and pineapple harvests necessitated the move to larger, more accessible facilities. Lahaina was more convenient for the new waves of workers responding to steadier supplies of pineapple and the peak summer harvests. In 1920, Honolua Ranch was renamed Baldwin Packers, and cannery operations moved to a new plant at Mālā Wharf in Lahaina.[7] The sugar cane trains of Pioneer Mill transported Honolua pineapples to the new cannery, and the old cannery in Honokahua closed.[8] With its land acquisitions burgeoning, the company had 22,600 acres in 1933.

People who lived in the village described it as a close-knit plantation community in which work, recreation, and life's passages took place within the ahupuaʻa. The school was small, the churches smaller, and activities revolved around the few amenities available: the Honolua Store, the mountains and beaches, a ball park, dairy, and the stable. When Wes Nohara attended Honokahua School, fewer than eighty children attended its classes from kindergarten through eighth grade. The older generations remember two classes in one room, sometimes more. Harry Pali, who died at eighty-four in 1996, told interviewer Shuji Seki that his father was the principal of a one-room school in Honokōhau Valley.[9] After the plantation headquarters were transferred to Honokahua, Pali walked a total of twelve miles a day between his home and the new school.[10]

"When I was young, we used to pick *hala* (pandanus) at Honokōhau," Pali told interviewer Lesley Bruce. "My mother used to weave lauhala mats for Mr. Fleming. My brother and I used to strip the leaves and put them in the parlor for her. Mr. Fleming asked her to make a mat, fourteen feet by fourteen feet.[11]

"Most of our things came from the land or ocean. We raised our own taro. Went down the beach fishing. And *hīhīwai* (freshwater shellfish)—used to get that too. We used to raise cabbage, and chickens, and get mango from the gulch and *pohole* (fern shoots) in Honokōhau Valley."

Master carver Sam Kaʻai, who lived for a time in Honokōhau Valley, had an uncle, Francis "Tito" Marciel, who was the village saddle-maker and meat-cutter.[12] "Tito Marciel did all the packaging and delivering of the meat," said Kaʻai. "He also made saddles and used to weave skin ropes. As teenagers, when we went to visit, we would first find out if he was weaving rope. If he was, we'd come out of the car. But if he wasn't, we knew he wanted us to saw logs, and we would run and hide. He always had logs to saw into slats for boards. The saw was always sharp, because he had melted waxed paper over its edge so it wouldn't rust."

Marciel, who was also the ranch policeman, made Hawaiian saddles by covering carved wood with leather. What blacksmithing the cowboys didn't do themselves, they left to the blacksmith shop at the company garage. "We just let the animals roam around," he told interviewer Lesley Bruce in 1978.[13] "The pasture goes from Mailepai all the way to Kahakuloa. There's plenty grass…We used to rope them and truck them to Kahului…then put them on the barge for Honolulu. We had Holstein cattle, but only a few employees got the milk. The doctor decided who needed the milk."

The milk was delivered on horse-drawn carts, which also carried water to the watermelon fields. The stables at Honokahua, where the beach is nicknamed Stables, were necessary because most people walked or rode horses in the pre-World War II years. Nohara's mother, who lived next door to his father, remembers her own mother walking two miles from Japanese Camp to Field 32 to work. "The village had to be close to the cannery and the fields because transportation was limited to horse or walking," he explained. "The task of caring for the fields was contracted out to families, and they were paid according to yields." Gasoline trucks were introduced after World War II as surplus equipment, and Nohara recalled seeing items from the war, such as helmets and Civil Defense supplies, stored at the dairy.

Camp residents did their own building and fixing, and Harry Pali recalled how the community worked together to build their churches. "We had this thing called MIA," he offered, "Mutual Improvement Association. The little church was filled. Everybody would come because there was nothing else to do, no TV, no movies."[14] There were three churches in the village, the Mormon, the Catholic, and the Reverend John Kukahiko's Honokahua Congregational Church.

In keeping with the plantation tradition of the time, Honolua Village was divided into residential "camps," loosely segregated by the workers' ethnicities and cultural traditions, or by simple geographic need:

Next page: The Honokahua Congregational Church, once led by the Reverend John Kukahiko, is now a preschool near D. T. Fleming Beach Park.

SILLA KAINA

Cultural Resources Coordinator, Kapalua Land Company

Sometimes we thought, 'Oh Dad, why did you live on the plantation?' But my mom always reminds us: he loved, he absolutely loved working for the company. We accepted the opportunity when the company decided to move the plantation down to Nāpili. We saw the changes. We also saw that you have to stand on your own. And we also saw the gratitude of my parents owning their first house together. That made a big difference. And so, even though we still lived in the area, we learned to accept these changes we saw around us.

People who worked for the plantation at that time knew that everything was for the company. I've had time to think of these things. My father must have really loved the company to give his whole life to it. We had many, many beautiful experiences. One of the highlights was when my father saw that the young boys here had no sports or physical areas for them to play in. So he created team sports—baseball for the boys and softball for the girls. There were different teams—slow-

pitch, mountain ball, he even had a nine-year-old girls' team, and that was my sisters, me, and other girls from the camp. He coached from the 1960s through the '70s. He wanted to do something to keep the boys out of mischief, and in creating these sports, he brought families together and helped better their lives.

We couldn't have made it with just the money from the camp people. That's when the teams were coming out with fancy jerseys. Before it was T-shirts and jeans, but now we had real softball outfits with nice socks and regular softball shoes. That's why we needed sponsors. One of our biggest sponsors was Maui Land & Pine, and Hawaiian Airlines would fly us to the other islands. We even had Tigers in the Pee Wee League, and even the supervisors and managers played and became coaches with my dad. They called us girls Nā Honokahua, and the boys were named Nā Honolua.

Hawaiian Camp, Japanese Camp, Filipino Camp, Kahauiki Camp, Māhinahina Camp, Coffee Ranch Village, Puerto Rican Camp (also known as Spanish Camp), and a few isolated outposts for those overseeing the maintenance of the Honolua Ditch. Silla Kaina, cultural resources coordinator for Kapalua Land Company, lived with her Hawaiian family in Japanese Camp. "My mom is from Hāna, and even she was amazed at how the some of the Japanese workers could speak fluent Hawaiian, even better than she could," Kaina marveled. "I recall one man that I always thought was Hawaiian, Mr. Harada. He spoke such good Hawaiian, but I found out that he was Japanese."

Kaina and Nohara are among former plantation residents who, as employees of ML&P or its subsidiary, Kapalua Land Company, have never left their childhood haunts. "Right here, this was Japanese Camp," Wes Nohara explained from the Kukui Room veranda on Office Road, where Kaina gives classes in Hawaiian crafts. "Everything mauka of Honolua Store and this area was Japanese Camp."

Henrietta Mahuna, who was transferred from the pineapple fields to Honolua Store in 1962, recalled with humor the predilections of the different ethnic groups when it came to food. "The Japanese only liked Japanese rice," she remembered. "No Hinode, no Kokeshi, just Kokusai from Japan." The wiry woman was able to hoist hundred-pound bags of rice, which she repackaged into ten- to twenty-pound portions in times of strike or ration.

The store's growth came in fits and spurts, but even the slow periods were productive for Mahuna. One disconcertingly quiet period spurred her into action. "The cash register was pulling in $80 to $90 a day," she worried. "How could you pay six people on that? The workers needed to eat. So I started the hot dog machine, and then stew and rice, and then started salting butterfish and beef briskets in five- and ten-gallon crocks." They sold so briskly that she expanded

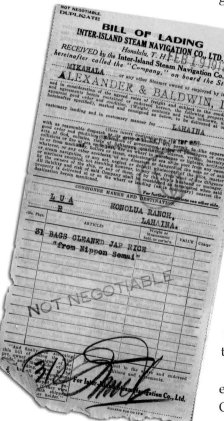

The Japanese workers at Honolua Village preferred rice from Japan.

the menu and began wrapping and steaming them, adding poi, laulau, ʻopihi, lomi salmon, and chicken long rice to the plate. Thus was born the Kapalua Hawaiian plate, a Friday special that consistently sold out at $5.50 each. On one particularly busy day, noted Mahuna, the kitchen served 400 people.

"She went full blast in the kitchen," added Orpha Kaina, who worked with Mahuna at the store. "We started a delivery service for people. We started selling material and more household things. People came from far away looking for things like poi strainers."

It was Mahuna's idea to install a washerette behind the store in the late 1960s, so residents would no longer have to tote their laundry ten miles to Lahaina. When visitors started flocking to Nāpili, she suggested to her boss that he buy a few cars and rent them, thus spawning the car rental business in northwest Maui. "In those days, we had to go outside and pump gas too," she added. "We had fun." For four of those early years, Mahuna boosted her business skills by commuting to Kahului for night classes at Maui Community College.

Mahuna's no-nonsense manner belied a soft heart that affected her customers' lives in ways they did not forget. "We had hippies, and I felt sorry for them when they didn't have money," she continued. "I used to go behind the boss's back and charge their laulau. They were all good kids. They always came back to pay, and they never forgot me. Today they have families and good jobs." When bawling children entered the store, her foolproof remedy was to briefly lead them into the walk-in refrigerator. Helpless parents were grateful, she said, and no child cried in the store after word got around.

"I was sassy, you know," she declared, long after her retirement in 1993.

Like Mahuna, Honolua Ranch and plantation Manager D. T. Fleming possessed energy and ingenuity that enhanced village life. His agricultural efforts and achievements were limitless. His outdoor life included polo, for which he kept his own stable, and his unwavering curiosity led him to plant dozens

of experimental crops in addition to pineapple. One of his experiments was aloe, the African succulent in the Liliaceae family with multiple medicinal benefits. In the early 1940s, he planted twenty-eight acres in Māhinahina, 'Alaeloa, and what later became known as Kapalua Resort.[15] He wrote to pharmaceutical companies hoping they would purchase and patent his formula, but he was too far ahead of his time.

"He took a lot of chances," commented the late Shuji Seki, who succeeded Fleming as postmaster of the village, and whose father managed the store at Honolua Bay and its present location on Office Road. "He was never afraid. He made that sunburn paste. I used it. He told me, 'Use it for your head and the hair will start growing again.' He saw me two to three months later. 'Well, sorry you're going to be bald-headed,' he told me." Fleming always kept a jar of aloe juice that he made in a special part of the cannery, Seki told an ML&P interviewer in 1984.[16]

No one who lived in Honolua Village could forget its characters or lifestyle. Even at eighty-eight years old, Kunio Kikuta still returns to the village, where three generations of his family lived and worked. "My father retired after forty years with the company, and I retired after thirty-three years," he said. "My two boys worked as truck drivers during summers, even after we moved to Kahului. When relatives visit us on Maui, we still take them to Honolua."

"We all grew up together, Wes and I and so many others," added Wayne Carroll, who moved to Honolua Village in 1957 at nine years old and retired after forty-two years with the company. "It was easy for all of us to work together. Nothing will ever compare to the plantation life. The plantation might have been segregated as far as the camps went, but probably in our era, a lot of that changed because of intermarriage. For us, there was no barrier to culture and getting along.

Above left: Residents of Hawaiian Camp prepare an *imu* to *kālua* a pig. *Above:* From the 1930s to '50s, D. T. Fleming worked with Stanford University and various laboratories to research aloe vera that he planted. He eventually gave up, saying it was too difficult to gain acceptance by the medical profession.

"While we were growing up, if there was a wedding or graduation or special event, it was guaranteed that all the different camps would donate their time," Carroll continued. "The kids took care of each other. The older kids would take care of the younger kids on the school bus, making sure that no one picked on them." Even in lean times, he said, a communal spirit prevailed, and the land always cooperated.

"If we were on strike, we'd form our own garden and fishing teams, and we'd fish for our soup kitchen," he continued. "We'd get together after work and do a little *lau* (surrounding the fish with a net) and distribute the fish among the families. We broke up into groups—those that were good *'opihi* (limpet) pickers, those who could fish, catch squid, pick limu (seaweed). And we'd share."

Seventy-five-year-old Isao Nakagawa, who retired as a shop supervisor after thirty-seven years with the company, is well known for his fishing skills. He remembered the days when employees would join in catching volumes of *akule*—big-eyed scad—and take

Left: Girls from Māhinahina Village rest on the weir of the Honolua Ditch. *Above:* Yosaku Shimomura from Japanese Village displays his catch of the day in 1935.

65

The Great Māhele of 1848 was the genesis of the transactions that would allow subjects of the Kingdom of Hawai'i to purchase and own land. Henry Perrine Baldwin purchased the lands that have evolved into Kapalua Resort, a development of Maui Land & Pineapple Company. Considered by many to be one of the more benevolent plantation owners of his time, H. P. Baldwin, with long-time manager D. T. Fleming, was the engine that powered the growth of the Honolua Ranch and plantation, the predecessor of ML&P.

He was the son of the Reverend Dwight Baldwin, a prominent Lahaina physician and missionary who had arrived with the Fourth Company of missionaries in 1831.[1] After the Great Māhele initiated private land ownership in the Hawaiian Islands, the Baldwins acquired large tracts of land, building upon a series of incremental land purchases made by H. P. Baldwin, and eventually, moving south along the coast, acquiring the ahupua'a of Māhinahina, Kahana, and others.

A man of modest beginnings, H. P. Baldwin was an East Maui plantation owner who changed the face of northwest Maui with his purchase of Honolua Ranch in 1889. Documents from the mid-1800s through early 1900s reveal a dizzying web of land transactions that began with the Hawaiian monarchy in the post-Māhele years. In 1855, King Kamehameha IV, Alexander Liholiho, awarded the 2,650-acre Honokahua ahupua'a to Kale Davis, the first-born daughter of Isaac Davis, one of two foreign advisers who were close confidants of Kamehameha I.[2] Bequeathed to Kale Davis's children, the ahupua'a was purchased in fragments by H. P. Baldwin. Parcel by parcel, he stitched together in the 1890s the enormous tracts of land that eventually became ML&P's Kapalua Resort, a master-planned community largely centered in the three ahupua'a of Honokahua, Honolua, and Honokōhau.[3] In 1889 Baldwin acquired the ahupua'a of Honolua, and, north of it, Honokōhau. Both were formerly owned by Kamehameha's great-grand-daughter, Ruth Ke'elikōlani. Baldwin made his purchases from Thomas Campbell, who owned the land after Princess Ruth and Samuel Parker.

Included in Baldwin's lands was a small parcel with a simple marker indicating the burial site of Kale Davis, the first landowner in Honokahua. Baldwin bought the parcel in 1894 from William Halstead, Davis's grandson, and the burial site is preserved today in an isolated area of Honokahua. Another significant acquisition was Honolua Ranch, with pastures, ranch headquarters, and employee housing straddling two ahupua'a in the lowlands near Honolua Bay. Richard C. Searle, the ranch manager, operated a small coffee plantation in the mountains but retired in 1911, thus creating an opportunity for a horticultural boom in the region.

David T. Fleming was the key to the greening of the land. He had been working in Ha'ikū for H. P. Baldwin and seemed the natural successor to Searle. Baldwin sagely tagged Fleming for Honolua, where Fleming began as manager on the first day of 1912. An enthusiastic planter, Fleming immersed himself in horticulture from the moment he took the reins, building upon Baldwin's extraordinary legacy after Baldwin died in July of 1911.

Maui historian Inez Ashdown, who wrote extensively about the Baldwins, described how H. P. Baldwin shared some life-altering wisdom with her father, Angus McPhee, who had lost his hand in a hunting accident. As the result of a gruesome mill accident, Baldwin had lost his right arm above the elbow, but he never let it slow him down. Said Baldwin to McPhee: "Young man, no doubt you feel that the world is finished for you, a cripple. Remember only that God gave us two hands in case we lose one!" From that day on, wrote Ashdown, her previously downcast father "never again gave way to regrets or self pity."[4]

Baldwin's resilience is also revealed in the memoir of his son, Arthur D. Baldwin. Upon approaching the mill for the first time after the accident, wrote the younger Baldwin, his father declared, "You have handicapped me for life. Now I am going to make you support me."[5]

When H. P. Baldwin and his partner, Samuel T. Alexander (with whom he formed Alexander & Baldwin Inc.), built the Hāmākua Ditch on the other side of the island, he "threw himself into the task" with undiminished energy, reports Arthur Baldwin. Before he had fully recovered from his horrific injury, H. P. Baldwin rappelled partway down a 200-foot cliff with his one arm, shaming the workmen out of their fear. He did this day after day, wrote Baldwin, "to keep the heart in them."[6]

Next page: Ruth Ke'elikōlani, great granddaughter of Kamehameha I, owned the ahupua'a of Honokōhau before H. P. Baldwin purchased it in the 1890s. It is now one of the three central ahupua'a of Kapalua Resort.

Know all men by these presents that we, Thomas Campbell and Helen A. Campbell his wife, of Paia Island of Maui Hawaiian Islands, for and in consideration of the sum of Thirty Five Thousand Dollars ($35000.00) to us in hand paid by Henry P. Baldwin of Haiku Maui, the receipt whereof is hereby acknowledged, have granted bargained sold and conveyed and by these presents do grant bargain sell and convey unto the said Henry P. Baldwin, his heirs, executors administrators and assigns all the following lands and property situated and being in the District of Kaanapali Island of Maui viz:

First   All that tract of Land known as the Ahupuaa of Honokohau according to its ancient boundaries as the same may be determined by the boundary Commission; being the same tract awarded to M. Kekuaiwa by Land Commission Award No. (9)

above written.

Witness
R. Brown

R. Keliikolani

their rewards home with them. Prompted by D. T. Fleming, an avid fisherman, the company had a commercial fishing operation with its own boats, nets and icehouse. It's said he built his home, Maka'oi'oi, on a bluff overlooking Moloka'i because it gave him a vantage point on his favorite fishing spot. Akule ran in massive schools there, and on a good day could be caught by the ton—four, five, even twelve—in the days before Honolua Bay was turned into a marine preserve.[17] Even on a work day, workers were allowed to leave their jobs when large schools were spotted in the bay. At the end of the day the catch was shared, but the weighing of the fish could continue late into the night.

"It depended on what kind of job you had," Nakagawa explained. "If you were a diver, you got a big amount of fish, and if you were a boatman, maybe less. And if you were just a net puller, well, you got maybe seven or eight fish." He described the truck going through the camps on the way to what was called the "ice mill," tooting its horn to announce the catch. "Even though we brought some akule home, I don't know why, but we would go back and buy some more," he continued. "That is why they had the ice mill below the store. We didn't have refrigerators, so we used to buy blocks of ice, which they would deliver. Everybody had a box for the ice, and that's why we called it 'icebox.'" Many people cleaned, salted and sun-dried their akule so it would last longer.

In April 1946, a tsunami hit West Maui and caused extensive damage to the Baldwin Packers cannery in Lahaina. In typewritten letters to H. A. Baldwin and Jack T. Waterhouse, Fleming described the damage in detail. "Once before, I saw water beyond control and I figured it was much worse than fire," Fleming wrote, "for in the last case, you can do something about it.

With water, the only thing to do is to get out as fast as you can, and wait until it has spent its force…

"One thing, fishing was really good out Honolua way yesterday—the best I ever saw. There were lovely Kenui, Kala, Palani, Pala, uu, etc., and eels by the dozen up in the Alfalfa patches. I saw one large Uu swimming around in the cannery, and outside of the cannery were plenty other fish, just waiting to be picked up."[18]

Through the years, declining revenues and fish prompted the company to discontinue its fishing operation in the mid-1950s, and in 1978, Honolua and Mokulē'ia bays were designated a marine life conservation district. While fish supplies were finite, the parks, beaches, and bays provided inexhaustible recreation and entertainment. In its early years, the company celebrated the end of each summer harvest with a picnic at Honolua Park. In more recent years, the Harvest Lū'au moved to Kapalua Beach, known in those days as Fleming's. A picture-perfect beach lined with coconut trees, Fleming's was an ideal venue with a pavilion, Boy Scouts campsite, and clear, gentle waters protected by rocky points at both ends of its white-sand crescent. Workers from Lahaina came by train to join the harvest celebrations in September, and there were games, an *imu* (underground rock oven), entertainment, and feasting aplenty.[19]

"Everybody participated in the annual Harvest Lū'au," remembered Kunio Kikuta. "Otherwise, throughout the year, when we had our individual activities, we celebrated among ourselves. There was wrestling and sumo, and mochi pounding was an annual event at New Year's." On May Day, students at Honokahua School gathered around a maypole in their prim white outfits and danced daintily until games of dodge ball and tug-of-war made their competitive

VALERIE HOʻOPAI

Human Resources Assistant, Kapalua Land Company

This was a very remote area when we were growing up. The only recreation we had was with our school activities, because our school was right here. After school, we had the garden to tend to, or brothers or sisters to play with, or our friends, our bicycles to ride, a basketball court, and the ocean. My mother would go down to one of the beaches down here and collect shells. And she made leis out of beautiful shells that are in the Niʻihau shell family, like a baby cone shell. She made shell leis for my sisters and my sister-in-law, and she also made one for me, but I didn't want it. I didn't realize how valuable it was, so it was given away. My sister-in-law has a six-strand lei that my mother made, and I know they are worth a lot of money. Those shells were easily found at one of these beaches. So, a couple of years ago, I went down to the same beach where she found these shells, and they're not there. They all left. That is one of the reasons I say that the old people have a lot of spirit and power, because when they die, things like that can die with them.

instincts roar. Throughout the year, employees and Boy Scouts troops from around the island camped, fished and snorkeled at Kapalua Beach.

In 1962, Baldwin Packers merged with Haleakala Pineapple Company, and three months later the company became Maui Pineapple Company, Ltd. Seven years later, the company experienced a tectonic shift when Colin Cameron, a fifth-generation Baldwin, became the first president of Maui Land & Pineapple Company, Inc. Cameron's extraordinary vision catapulted the company's interests into larger dimensions: Kapalua Resort, a harmonious union of hospitality, stewardship, and the environmental excellence inherent in the region. For the community, this meant the gradual relocation of the residents and the dismantling of the camps. In the 1960s and '70s, as resort planning and construction began, residents from the camps experienced the bittersweet process of moving to new employee housing in nearby Nāpilihau.

Valerie Hoʻopai, who grew up in Hawaiian Camp, remembers her childhood this way: "We grew our gardens. The water was free. Many of us paid rent— below $25 for the whole house—until we moved out in 1974. My daughter lived here for two or three years, and my husband speared his first fish here. This was where he learned to surf. My father never had much of an education, but he had a lot of skills. He could kālua a pig. He was a great fisherman.

"There were a lot of things that the old people had power in. They had spiritual power, and they also had power to deal with the spirit of the land and the mountains. My parents somehow had that. It was not something to brag about; they just had it."

Paradise
FOUND

Preceding page: Clear water, a reef that protects against strong currents, and a view of Moloka'i make Kapalua Beach a stellar West Maui attraction. *This page:* The view of Lāna'i from Nāmalu Point has many moods and faces.

"Please accept my heartiest congratulations on the opening of Kapalua Bay Hotel and our very best wishes for its outstanding success in the years ahead," read the RCA telegram. "You can be justifiably proud of this magnificent new hotel and we can look forward to visiting with you there in the near future."[1] The telegram, sent October 13, 1978, was from Laurance Rockefeller, the noted philanthropist, conservationist, and financier, as he congratulated the late Colin C. Cameron upon opening the Kapalua Bay Hotel on the shores of northwest Maui.

Rockefeller's company, RockResorts, had developed the Mauna Kea Beach Hotel on the island of Hawai'i and was chosen to manage the new Kapalua Bay Hotel in 1976. The hotel was a pioneer in the resort world, a dream come true for Colin Cameron, who, as the great-grandson of H. P. Baldwin, had a genetic disposition to taking great leaps of the imagination. While he did not rappel down a cliff with one arm, as his great-grandfather did, Cameron possessed an inspired sense of possibility and the patience to go with it. As president and chairman of Maui Land & Pineapple Company, Inc., which he founded in 1969, Cameron took bold steps toward defining the next generation of change in northwest Maui.

Where plantation laborers had eked out a living since the early 1900s, he envisioned luxury hotels in a master-planned resort. Where horse-drawn carts had once irrigated watermelon and pineapple fields, he

visualized golf carts on a conservation-minded golf course. And where Boy Scouts and plantation families had camped and snorkeled at the old Fleming's Beach, he imagined international travelers as new members of the community. Cameron took a leap to implement his vision, and in the process built a bridge to the future.

In the 1960s, the Baldwin family's enterprises took a turn in the road that led to northwest Maui. Baldwin Packers had merged with Maui Pineapple Company in 1962 and united the Baldwin family's East Maui and West Maui operations. As executive vice president of the resulting company, Maui Pineapple Company, Inc., Cameron foresaw the future. "Even then I felt there was a real potential for development and future use of some of those lands," he told interviewer Nancy Markel in the fall of 1974.[2] "Beach front lands, the Ka'anapali Amfac development, were just getting under way. You could see, down the line, an opportunity for the future Maui to develop."

Cameron formed ML&P following a buyout of Maui Pineapple Company from Alexander & Baldwin Inc. in 1969 "after a longstanding feud over its management," reported *Hawaii Business* magazine in May 1989.[3] Cameron told interviewer Nancy Markel that his family favored keeping the operations headquartered on Maui rather than moving them to Honolulu. "I think the community of Maui has been very good to us," he told Markel. "Hopefully, some of the things that we have done in a very broad sense are good for the community also."[4] The purchase was made partly with cash and partly by exchanging A&B stock, and the result, Maui Land & Pineapple Company, was a publicly held company with Cameron as its first president.[5]

Kapalua Land Company, Ltd., a wholly owned subsidiary of ML&P, responded to the times and launched the company into the new world. Statehood for Hawai'i had set the stage for tourism a decade earlier, and jet travel had catapulted the state into the international arena. "With all the excitement about the arrival of statehood that year, many barely noticed that a technological revolution also landed at Honolulu International [Airport] with a new, reliable Boeing 707, the first all-jet passenger plane," wrote Robert W. Bone in *Hawai'i ka 'oihana hōkele*, a commemorative edition of the Hawai'i Hotel Association.[6] Jet travel heralded a new era, continued Bone, "in which tourism in Hawaii was no longer just a local affair."

As president of ML&P, Cameron was in a position to merge his interests into one cohesive whole: a hotel, resort, and residential community in a working plantation, surrounded by nature and united by a respect for the environment and a commitment to responsible stewardship. The environmental features alone were staggering. A coastline of soaring beauty was shaped by a string of historically and culturally significant bays facing Moloka'i and Lāna'i. Pu'u Kukui, the summit of the West Maui Mountains, was its mauka equivalent, an ecosystem of rare native vegetation and valleys sculpted by streams and waterfalls. In all directions rolled a carpet of green—23,000 acres of land, most of it in open space, the country's largest working pineapple plantation. As directed by the company's credo, all development would conform to the natural terrain.

Two hotels were planned for the high-end destination, each with an 18-hole golf course surrounded by tasteful residences. The company created employee housing in nearby Nāpilihau, and the plantation families slowly vacated Honolua Village in preparation for Kapalua Resort. Kapalua Land Company, Ltd. was incorporated in 1975 to oversee the development of Kapalua Resort, a destination with cultural, historical, and environmental elements unequalled in Hawai'i.

"Was there any question in your mind what kind of developing you wanted to do?" Nancy Markel of Hall & Levine Advertising asked Cameron in the fall of 1974, while preparing an advertising campaign for Kapalua Resort. "Did you always know that you wanted a quality development?"[7]

"Exactly what would be built, no, I didn't know anything about this business when I started," Cameron replied. "I've had a lot of education over the years and it's been quite costly, and through various consultants, I've learned something. You might say that I've gotten another degree in Resort Development."

The Harvard-educated Cameron was modest in his self-assessment. "I always thought I would come back and work in the pineapple business, even though I didn't know a heck of a lot about it," he reflected. "I worked for the company in the summers and took some courses at school which were related [to agriculture] either directly or indirectly, but I didn't pull myself up as an expert, or even an engineer. I always like to have long-term goals and objectives…Where do I want this company to be, or parts of this development to be, five or ten years from now? What are the trends, what can I see happening? What are we trying to accomplish, where are we trying to go? I try to combine that with extreme flexibility in the short term."

Kapalua, meaning "two borders," was chosen as the name for the resort.[8] Poetically interpreted, the name means "arms embracing the sea," an apt description of the lava promontories bordering the crescent-shaped Kapalua Beach. The volcanic outcroppings appear to be cradling the white-sand beach, reaching out to the sea. Formerly Fleming's Beach, Kapalua, writes cultural historian Kepā Maly, was identified as early as 1854 as a place near the shore on the boundary of Honokahua.[9]

Ground was broken for the $20-million, 196-room Kapalua Bay Hotel in 1976. Citing H. P. Baldwin and D. T. Fleming as the pioneers of the resort, Cameron told the gathering, "All these trees that you see…the Cook pines…the pineapple…were brought here because the two men were pioneers—bold and daring, ahead of their times. And it was fifteen years ago that I first walked this site and thought, what a great place for a hotel. Kā'anapali was just getting started then. And I think I can safely say if my great grandfather and D. T. Fleming could see this now—they'd be pleased."[10]

The Bay Villas, Kapalua Land Company's first condominium project, opened that year, followed by The Golf Villas the next year. They sold so quickly, reported the May, 1989 *Hawaii Business* magazine, "that Cameron was forced to set up a lottery system to decide who would win the privilege of purchasing the $134,000 units."[11] Kapalua Bay Hotel opened in 1978, the same year that Honolua and Mokulē'ia bays were declared marine-life sanctuaries.

From architecture to marketing, and even at its opening, when swarms of fruit flies bombarded the lobby, the hotel was rife with problems. Correcting the flaws was costly, and by 1984, ML&P was $52 million in debt.[12] Cameron ended his management contract with RockResorts and sold the hotel in 1985 to employee Mark Rolfing and his partners.

Through the years, new amenities brought thoughtful recreation and the lightest of footprints to Kapalua Resort. Three golf courses, The Village, The Bay, and The Plantation courses, added new horizons of green, each adhering to the resort's conservation ethic as a "Certified Audubon Cooperative Sanctuary." Honolua Village went from being the hub of a plantation to the heart of a plantation-themed resort village, and a new community began to take shape. In 1988, a decade after the Kapalua Bay Hotel opened on Kapalua Bay, the Pu'u Kukui Watershed was established as a conservation benchmark, raising the bar again on the practice of responsible stewardship.

For ML&P, 1992 was a year of dramatic passages, marked by three major events bringing tectonic shifts to the company. ML&P dedicated Pu'u Kukui Preserve to The Nature Conservancy of Hawai'i. The Ritz-Carlton, Kapalua opened, introducing new levels of elegance,

stewardship, and cultural sensitivity from its perch above Honokahua Bay. But when Colin Cameron died of a heart attack at sixty-five years old, the company he had led for twenty-three years suddenly found itself rudderless.

It took a few years for the leadership vacuum to be filled, and in the interim, the company remained stable but unprofitable, adhering to the status quo. When the company assumed a new direction, the velocity of the shift was breathtaking. Hawai'i-born Steve Case, founder of America Online, bought a controlling interest in ML&P and raised the curtain on a new era for the company and the Maui community. When his friend and colleague, former AOL executive David Cole, became president and CEO of ML&P in 2003, the energy acceleration was palpable.

Cole brought new meaning to the words "agriculture" and "sustainability" and a mature activism to the company. With what the *Honolulu Advertiser* described as "an unlikely combination of technology and organic farming experience," Cole redefined the company's direction and, in eloquent speeches and newspaper commentaries, put under scrutiny Hawai'i's ecological practices and dependence on imported fuel and food.[13] After moving from his Sunnyside Farms in Virginia to his former home, Hawai'i, Cole became a visible force in promoting sustainable agriculture and linking it with tourism in ways Hawai'i had not seen before.

"A new future for ML&P," read the leading *Maui News* headline on March 26, 2004. "Entrepreneurial agriculture to replace old plantation style."[14] Cole's vision was described as "holistic," involving a retooling of the company's West Maui holdings. The new direction would enlarge Pu'u Kukui's conservation area, step up local organic food production, and integrate tourism, housing, renewable energy, and sustainable agriculture in a lifestyle rooted in Hawaiian values. In short, the future had arrived in the form of David Cole.

But there were tough decisions along the way. One of them was the dismantling of the Marriott-operated Kapalua Bay Hotel, which ML&P had sold

A view from Honolua Ridge shows
Moloka'i on a calm, crisp morning.

in 1985 and repurchased in 2004. As part of a much-needed renaissance of Kapalua Resort, the hotel was demolished in April 2006, to be replaced by an upscale, residential, members-only beachside club—The Ritz-Carlton Club and Residences, Kapalua Bay—managed by the Ritz-Carlton Hotel Company.[15] When the action was criticized, Cole underscored the importance of serving the needs of up-market customers capable of weathering down-market cycles.

While the razing of the hotel was controversial, the "upcycling" of the materials in the former hotel was lauded as exemplary. The *New York Times*, in an article on Cole and the Hawai'i BioEnergy consortium he co-founded, reported that "This year, when construction crews dismantled the former Kapalua Bay Hotel…Mr. Cole required them to reuse 97 percent of the material in the company's new offices. Instead of recycling, he called the process 'upcycling,' and noted that his desk was a door in its former life."[16]

Throughout much of 2007, Kapalua Resort hummed with the signs of reconstruction. Following a six-month, $160-million renovation, The Ritz-Carlton, Kapalua hotel reopened with a flourish in December 2007, in time for the annual Mercedes-Benz Championship, the champions-only PGA TOUR golf tournament. Having acquired an ownership interest in the newly retooled Ritz-Carlton, Kapalua, ML&P ended the year as a bigger stakeholder than ever. The fearlessness of the company's founder, H. P. Baldwin, was reincarnated in the form of a twenty-first-century business leader and conservationist.

"Our job is to fashion the future," said Cole. "And I believe that while we have to be concerned with short-term issues, we're obligated, first and foremost, to having a long-term view of the value we're creating for our employees, our customers, our shareholders, and the public."

Committed to what he calls "values-driven management," Cole implemented a comprehensive program, built on three core Hawaiian values, for planting the seeds for the company's next century: *ho'ohanohano*, conducting oneself with distinction; *mālama 'āina*, protecting, preserving, and caring for the land; and *po'okela*, creating excellence and superior workmanship. In corporate vernacular, these terms would translate to equity, ecology, and economy.

"I didn't bring these values, but I led a process with prominent employees to rediscover them," he noted. These values have spawned numerous initiatives, including recycling and "upcycling" efforts, organic crops, and a native koa reforestation program.

Covering hundreds of acres of buffer lands between the resort and sensitive mauka lands, the trees will reach maturity in twenty-five to thirty years. The plan also calls for an additional zone of permanent native forest between the koa plantings and the Pu'u Kukui Watershed Preserve.

"The first hardwoods will be harvested in 2035," continued Cole. "Our planning horizon must stretch for decades and beyond, because our 'āina requires this of us. We have the largest and best-managed private preserve in the state, and we are making it larger to ensure that our natural community can thrive long after we are gone.

"In return, we have the rare privilege of experiencing the true beauty and mystery of Hawai'i."

Cornucopia

Before plastic and supermarkets, food came straight from the ground. There was little distance between the farm and the plate. Sunshine, water, birds and bees, with a few seeds and a boost of elbow grease, could produce the makings of a brilliant repast. Taro clung to valley floors, and coconut palms, filled with nectar, were fountains in the air. Trees hung heavy with fruit. The ocean was the fish market, abundant and self-sustaining due to the Hawaiian practice of harvesting seasonally to conserve precious marine resources.

Charlie Dofa comes from the old school of gardening: that less is more, that fresh is good, that organic is better still. Every day after work, you can find him in the sun, on a hill, in his little patch of heaven, watering and pruning his leafy world. His face is joyful and his hands are dirty, and all around him, his plants are growing at warp speed. The eggplants are the size of melons. The carrots are as sweet as apples. Maui onions, white squash, Okinawan sweet potatoes, broccoli, okra, cucumbers, lettuce—it's a garden worthy of the gods. His garden plot, ten by twenty feet, is surrounded by a bamboo trellis, with seeds germinating in a corner, tall corn waving at the borders, and stepping stones built of rocks from nearby fields. At the entrance to the garden complex, adding a special aesthetic feature, Dofa has built a wall of basalt, each stone perfectly secured and stable without the use of cement.

"This is our community garden," beamed Dofa. "Everyone gives their _kōkua_ [helps] here. Everybody has to pull a few weeds before harvest. Each employee has a plot, and it's all organic. I use chicken and horse manure, and blood meal, bone meal, and fish emul-

sion. We can't use chemicals, we can't spray or use anything to kill the bugs. I water my garden, and when I can't do anything else, I take a run. Then I come back and see if there are weeds to be pulled." Dofa is a five-time marathon finisher and the unofficial captain of the garden community, with more than enough energy for his own plot of paradise and for helping his neophyte neighbors.

The Kapalua community gardens are a patchwork of forty-one plots, each ten by twenty feet, on a half-acre of land set aside for ML&P's West Maui employees. With land and water provided by the company, and strict rules for organic management, the gardens fulfill multiple purposes and many appetites.

"We made these community gardens available to our employees to help them understand organic farming, and to give them a plot where they can grow their own produce for home consumption," explained Wes Nohara, general manager of Kapalua Farms. "We are also working with schools to teach their youth about organic farming and business management. This reflects our ties to the community, to our employees, to our company business plan in terms of producing high-quality organic produce for our resort and building a model of sustainable agriculture."

Around the community gardens are the rolling fields of Kapalua Farms, the cornucopia of the resort. The twenty-acre farm for diversified organic crops is just the beginning of a seventy-five-acre commitment. More than fifty acres have been allocated for organic pineapple, with another five acres for nursery work and composting. The long-term plans keep the farm in

Preceding pages: Pineapple fields, Cook pines, and rainbows are abundant at Kapalua Resort.
Left: Organic Swiss chard is one of many vegetables grown at Kapalua Farms and available at Honolua Store's outdoor market.

TOVA CALLENDER

Diversified Agriculture Supervisor

We all think we've got the best jobs ever because we get to be on the leading edge. Kapalua Farms is needed for many different reasons, especially here in Hawai'i, because food self-sufficiency is so sorely needed.

We are organically managed while using organic practices that go a step beyond organic, because organic doesn't necessarily mean sustainable. Our farm is sustainable.

We make our own compost. If you are organically certified but import all of your soil amendment—fertilizer, or lime, or whatever pest management program you're dealing with—there are still different agricultural products to choose from, and a lot of them are mined. Most fertilizers come from mined sources, and that is a devastating process for the environment. People now recognize that organic is not enough, and we're taking that important extra step.

a state of creative flux: workers are researching organic pineapple, creating their own compost, and planting an extensive selection of fresh, organically managed produce for the hotels, resort restaurants, and the Thursday produce stand at Honolua Store. In growing numbers, resort residents, hotel guests, and members of the local community gather at Honolua Store to stock up on the diverse fresh produce grown at Kapalua Farms.

"There is a mix of people who shop at the Thursday market," explained Tova Callender, diversified agriculture supervisor of Kapalua Farms. "There are people who have residences and are part of the neighborhood, who have been coming here for twenty years. There are employees, from hourly workers to golf maintenance, all the way to the upper management of the company, who buy their fresh produce here weekly. Honolua Store is a wonderful place where people from all parts of the community can gather and interact."

Aromatic herbs, vine-ripened tomatoes, yellow wax beans, Malabar spinach, carrots, chard, leeks, figs, several varieties of beets, Maui onions, fresh-shelled peas, and a rainbow of produce, picked within the hour, beckon from baskets and bins, to be scooped up at reasonable prices. Fruit, from liliko'i and papaya to ML&P's signature pineapple, add sweetness to the selection. "We're also experimenting with citrus, lemon, lime, orange, rambutan, avocado, litchi, acerola, figs, cacao, and other fruit crops, and it's very exciting," explained Callender.

Maui Land & Pineapple Company's Maui Gold brand, introduced in 2005, is the pride of the company, a sumptuous premium pineapple with taste, texture, and nutritional qualities that have catapulted it to the top of the culinary heap. Maui's warm days, cool nights, hillside elevation, sweet, fresh water, and fertile volcanic soil combine to create an extraordinary variety considered by many to be superior to any other on the market. Only the top-of-the-line pineapples with a flawless appearance and straight crowns

Next page: Only top-quality pineapples are sold as the sweet, low-acid Maui Gold, higher than the norm in vitamin C and bromelain.

are marketed as Maui Gold. Pineapples that fail to meet these high aesthetic standards are sold to food service institutions under the Hawaiian Gold label, while other sub-standard fruit are destined for the juice market. Sweet and juicy and low in acid, Maui Gold is the crowning glory of ML&P's agricultural offerings. High in bromelain, the digestive enzyme with strong anti-inflammatory properties, and containing three times more vitamin C than the conventional Smooth Cayenne pineapple, Maui Gold is also nutritious, ideally suited to the tastes and lifestyle of the Kapalua Resort community.

Three thousand acres of this cross-pollinated hybrid are under cultivation. Since June 2007, when low-cost foreign competition prompted ML&P to close its pineapple canning operations in Kahului, Maui, the popular Maui Gold has taken center stage as the centerpiece of its specialty fresh fruit operations.

Kapalua Farms is developing an organic form of the fruit that will be marketed as Kapalua Gold. In its commitment to sustainable agriculture, Kapalua Farms devotes considerable energy and resources to nurturing its products from the soil up, in a complete cycle of regeneration.

"We take people's lawn clippings, grass cuttings, what they prune from their trees, things that would normally go into a landfill, and we chop it into fine piles instead of taking it to the landfills," explained Nohara. "This material contains a lot of carbon. We try to break down that carbon, bond it with some nitrogen, and break it down further with oxygen and moisture. Then it forms something like a soil, a nutrient-rich, naturally produced material." The material is provided as organic compost for the community gardens and is combined with other material for larger-scale farming.

Nohara pointed to the yellow flowers of the Sunn Hemp. "This is a nitrogen-fixing plant," he explained. "We use this for intercropping. You put in the compost, and it changes the entire composition of the soil and enhances its environment. It's much friendlier to

earthworms and other organisms in the soil. A healthy soil should have minerals, which is the broken-down volcanic rock, and it should have animals, good ones and detrimental ones, and it also needs vegetative matter." In good soil, he said, the acidity is balanced and the nutrients are reduced to a form that plants can use most efficiently.

"Think of the soil as a bank, and you've just made a huge deposit into your bank account. When you grow a plant, you're withdrawing from your bank account, but you cannot continue withdrawing without replenishing. This puts the nutrients back in and makes them more available so the plants can grow healthier and faster."

Nohara could barely conceal his excitement as he surveyed the lands makai of the community gardens. "We have a team researching the best farm practices for organic pineapple," he continued. "For a new product or a new method, it's a good idea to work in a small environment. That's what this is about. These gardens are our test plots for organic pineapple and our chefs' kitchens. We also plan orchards of organic fruits and vegetables and offer a walking tour so the community can observe what we're doing." An edible-landscape demonstration garden and a one-acre Hawaiian ethno-botanical garden are also in the works, along with a garden of bromeliads.

Fueled by these initiatives, a distinctive culinary signature has emerged at Kapalua Resort. Through the farm-to-table connection, chefs have top-drawer, fresh ingredients worthy of their skills and imaginations. Throughout the resort community, artisanal products are more than a menu highlight or a pleasing dining experience. They are an integral part of an authentic experience, an exchange of culture and values between host and guest.

Leading the charge is ML&P CEO David Cole, a man of extraordinary intellect. The current chairman of The Nature Conservancy of Hawai'i, Cole has the ability to translate lofty principles into action from the ground up. Positioning Maui Gold at the apex of the pineapple world is no quixotic pursuit for him, nor is the goal of creating a sustainable community. At every opportunity, Cole can be heard lamenting Hawai'i's dire statistics: that just over one-tenth of Hawai'i's food is grown in the Islands, and that fresh food supplies would last a mere four days in the event of a disaster.[1]

"By tapping into the principles of self-reliance that we learned as children of Hawai'i, and candidly assessing the lessons of overdependence on remote forces, we may be the world's best hope for demonstrating how communities can thrive by blending island consciousness with intelligent use of our sunlight, soils and waters," he wrote in the *Honolulu Advertiser* on April 22, 2007. "Before the introduction of jet aircraft and cheap fuel 50 years ago, we lived a largely self-reliant lifestyle where agriculture reigned as our leading industry, and we lived with a heightened sense of our 'islandness.' Our fish came from nearby shores and our vegetables came from local farmers. We understood intuitively that our Islands were a closed ecosystem; and we knew if we took care of them, they would take care of us. *Mālama 'āina*."[2]

Clockwise from top right: Egg-plants, carrots, green onions, and Maui Gold pineapples are among the premium fresh products grown at Kapalua Farms.

CHARLES DOFA

Heavy Equipment Operator, The Plantation Course

The kids who come here with their families call me 'Uncle Charlie.' I show them how to prepare the ground, read the package of seeds, keep tilling the ground until you're tired, and then plant the seeds. I teach them to keep moisture on the seeds while they germinate. When they see their first harvest, their eyes get big and they're yelling, 'Oh, I like this!'

If you've never gardened before, it's quite a feeling to see something grow, something you've tended, something that you didn't buy from the store. Tomatoes, lettuce, beans, eggplants, radishes—these products are expensive in the market. I have been here for thirty years, and this is something you can't refuse: free water, free land, plus a gate.

For some of the employees, this is the first time they're getting their hands dirty. Everyone works hard for the company. This is where they can come to relax; it's good therapy. And when you grow organic, the food tastes better, and you can tell the difference. It might not be a bigger vegetable, but it's more 'ono.

Sustainable living, Cole has said repeatedly, "is in Hawai'i's DNA."

Toward that end, ML&P puts a high premium on education and cultural exchange. Callender works with schools and community outreach programs and is helping to establish a green market similar to the one at Honolua Store, this time in upcountry Maui. Local efforts include a program to include gardens as part of the Maui school curriculum, and international exchanges are also underway. Graduates and scholars from Costa Rica's Earth University, a four-year entrepreneurial and agricultural college, work on Maui as farm coordinators for Kapalua Farms.

The wholeness of the cycle, the entirety of growth, pleasure, consumption, decline, and regeneration, can be seen in the simple plots of earth at the community gardens of Kapalua Farms. Charlie Dofa makes his daily stop at his bountiful patch of green. He wastes no time in checking his seedlings and watering the rows of eggplants, beans, lettuces, and squash, harvesting what is ready for his family's repast. His neighbor's sunflowers dance in the wind. As the sun sinks in the sky, he pauses to admire his handiwork. "It's about time I planted the beans, the long Filipino beans," he declares. "The tomatoes, eggplant, bell peppers, and Hawaiian chili peppers are the ones that grow fast. The cucumbers will be ready soon. And if you like flowers, sunflowers and daisies grow well." He plucks a radish from the ground, rinses it, and tucks into it with a crunch. "This is good," he murmurs. "Straight from the ground. You don't need much more than this."

In his essay, "Communities of Food," Carlo Petrini put it this way: "In producing food locally, people adopt the habits that shorten the distance between the producer and the consumer, that contribute to the well-being of the community, that help those who work in the fields to prosper, that give health, that give beauty to their own land…

"The land is our common home."[3]

Next page: Local organic products and creative chefs are the main ingredients in Kapalua's dining rooms.

The Global
VILLAGE

"When I wake up on Maui, I am so aware of being alive," said George Mackin, a publishing executive who divides his time between Los Angeles and Kapalua Resort. "This is my sanctuary, my world, the place where I most want to exist, on so many levels—spiritually, emotionally, and physically. When I wake up in Kapalua I am so glad to be alive, I just celebrate each day. It's a combination of celebrating the immediate environment, which I can do in a hundred different ways, and doing something physically fulfilling, like hiking, tennis, swimming, golf, or just loving my family. Kapalua continually redefines all my senses."

Mackin, the owner of *Tennis Magazine*, has owned various residences at Kapalua Resort for the past fifteen years. When he is not traveling or in Los Angeles, he spends time at his home in The Plantation Estates, his mountain idyll at the foot of Pu'u Kukui, the largest privately owned nature preserve in the Hawaiian Islands. He opens the windows in the morning, smells the fresh ocean and mountain air, takes in the views from Pu'u Kukui to Honolua Bay, and ponders his next step. "I do something that gets my sensory being charged up," he said. "A swim in the pool, maybe the ocean, or just standing outside and feeling the Hawaiian trade winds cleanse my soul. I usually start with a fresh Hawaiian breakfast, and from there, each day is a white canvas—never typical, always engaging—for me to paint."

While Pu'u Kukui is a large natural backdrop, Mackin's day is measured in small, immediate moments—moments of clarity and fulfillment, to be savored as brush strokes on the canvas of his day, the

creative expression of a lifestyle. Like many other residents and visitors, Mackin considers West Maui his place of empowerment, a place where the natural environment supports his existence and clears the lens through which he views the rest of life and the world. His paradise may not be portable, but the qualities it engenders are. In planning for the next 100 years, those charting the future of Kapalua Nui strive to plant the seeds of joy and awe that they recognize in people like him.

As those plans materialize and a new way of life emerges, the words of William McDonough and Michael Braungart come to mind: "Strive for 'good growth,' not just economic growth," they write in *Cradle to Cradle*, their seminal book on eco-effective design. "Think of…designs in general as seeds. Such seeds can take all manner of cultural, material, and even spiritual forms."[1]

While the Hawaiians left their mana in the soil of Honokahua, the plantation workers left their own unshakable imprint, a fortitude forged by hardship and buoyed by a wondrous environment. Springing from this cultural milieu is the blueprint for a fresh and achievable utopia: villages, a town, eco-conscious recreation, sustainable food supplies, and hotels and residences in thoughtfully designed communities. The broad canvas for this creation is the 23,000-acre Kapalua Nui, where a new way of life is sprouting, bordered by two peerless natural sanctuaries: the Pu'u Kukui Watershed Preserve in the mountains, and a marine preserve, the Honolua-Mokulē'ia Marine Life Conservation District, at the shore.

Preceding pages: With its signature Cook pines and Moloka'i across the channel, Kapalua—"arms embracing the sea"—is flanked by marine and nature preserves. *Left:* Pu'u Kukui's brooding mysteries are fleetingly unveiled.

The fifth hole of The Bay Course shows why golf and recreation are major attractions at Kapalua Resort.

"We are opening up our lands for the enjoyment of residents and guests," explained Ryan Churchill, senior vice president of corporate development for Maui Land & Pineapple Company, the parent company of Kapalua Land Company. "We're creating a place in which to live and play, and we're introducing features that have not been previously available, such as a spa, a beach club, and various amenities in the mountains. We are essentially opening up our 23,000 acres, including some areas that were previously inaccessible, so residents will have everything they need in Kapalua without having to drive elsewhere."

Luxury amenities, such as homes and residences, are tailored to various environments, looking out upon bays, ridges, mountain slopes, Lāna'i and Moloka'i across the channels. What began as a single residential community, The Bay Villas, has blossomed into ten, with two golf courses and another on the way, a golf academy, a tennis complex, and a loyal base of community members who, like Mackin, revel in the amenities and their soulful connection to the place. They fill their days with fine dining, sports, snorkeling, kayaking…or simply nothing. They get fit and stay fit by bicycling or hiking on the emerging increments of a 100-mile trail system through the mountainous hinterlands, or along the 11.5-mile coastal trail where the great chief Pi'ilani watched from the cliffs for invaders in the sixteenth century.

"This is its own national park," continued Churchill. "Our goal is always understated elegance, being true to the history of the area, with plantation-style architecture throughout the village and in the

way we retain the identity of this place. Rather than changing these features, we're adapting them to the modern lifestyle." Places to live, villages to gather in, wilderness to explore, the ocean for recreation and inspiration—these are the layers of the exalted lifestyle that defines Kapalua Resort.

Sustainable agriculture, stewardship of natural resources, and ecologically effective design principles are three of the elements that inspire and inform the development. But they are just the starting points. To the healing ocean environment comes a seaside spa rooted in the timeless traditions of island plants and minerals. Small retail operations and tree-shaded promenades for strolling and lingering anchor plantation-styled village centers. From its ironwood-shaded perch above Honokahua Bay, The Ritz-Carlton, Kapalua, newly unveiled after a $160-million renovation, continues its tradition of excellence with its twelfth consecutive AAA Five-Diamond award. Throughout the resort, the human presence, in the form of architecture, planning, service, and design, leaves a tiny footprint in the vast landscape that is Kapalua Nui.

The Ritz-Carlton, Kapalua is located in The Village at Kapalua, a twenty-first-century incarnation of the plantation village where generations of workers lived and played between punishing bouts of labor in the Honokahua cannery and the surrounding fields of pineapple. The Honolua Store opened in 1929 and quickly became the nexus of what was then known as Honolua Village. It has never lost its humble luster, its grip on people's hearts. Guests, employees, residents, and even casual passersby still consider it to be the heart of the resort. With its sense of nostalgia, plantation architecture, and convivial, gregarious environment, it's the communal living room of Kapalua Resort. People shop for supplies, stock up on organic produce at the Thursday produce stands, and enjoy breakfast or lunch on the veranda. Local values—ties to community, heritage, and island culture—merge there with a sophisticated global population and become a powerful dynamic in the people's daily life. Across the parking

lot, international travelers arrive and depart in the welcoming plantation architecture of the resort's reception area.

Next door, the cultural center, The Kukui Room, enlivens village life with programs in Hawaiian crafts that use plant materials gathered from the neighborhood. From its exhibits of Hawaiian and plantation artifacts, the genealogy of the resort can be gleaned and its cultural matrix revealed. Hula lessons and classes in indigenous plants impart knowledge of place and history. On the veranda, a stone's throw from her childhood home in Honolua's Japanese Camp, Cultural Resources Coordinator Silla Kaina shares the depth of her love for her culture with lauhala weaving, lei making, and a good dose of *mo'olelo*, the stories of the region.

Connecting the mauka-to-makai communities is an intricate network of roads and trails for multiple uses and modes of transportation: vehicles, small resort shuttles, bicycles, and those with the smallest footprint, the hikers. Access around the conservation lands is controlled to protect the ecosystem, and the trails are designed with natural surfaces, from rugged to paved, to match the level of use. Although it is wise to watch one's footing on the remote mountain trails, it's impossible to avert the eyes from the ubiquitous panoramic vistas. The views of the coastline, of the Bays of Pi'ilani and the islands of Lāna'i and Moloka'i, are humbling in their splendor. Higher on the mountain, in the Pu'u Kukui Watershed Preserve, tree canopies veil the sky and the *'i'iwi* and *'apapane*, the delicate Hawaiian honeycreepers, chirp and flit through the tree tops in search of nectar to sip with their curved beaks.

Their venue—the air—is the new medium of recreation at the 1,200-to-1,800-foot elevation. On a two-mile zipline course mauka of the resort, guests soar silently above the tree canopy, ravines, and foliage for the headiest view of all: the coastline as seen from the air, off the ground, off the earth, in the sublime heights of Mauna Kahalawai. Adventurers travel 15 to 150 feet off the ground, on one of the longest systems of its kind

Nature lovers take a day trip in the Pu'u Kukui Watershed Preserve.

in North America. Guides for the Kapalua Adventure Center and Mountain Outpost are trained in the geology, culture, and natural history of the area, and all aspects of the program are designed for minimal impact on the ecosystem. Biodiesel-fueled Mercedes-Benz Unimogs transport guests to the site, and much of the experience is wheelchair-accessible. The course is in Waikulu, "trickling water," with Honokōhau at its northern border and Honokahua to the south.

The cultural and environmental effects of introducing this course to the environment were not taken lightly. Paths are designed to minimize erosion, and sensitive areas are avoided. In preparing for the mountain adventure, the resort invited the *mana'o*, the ideas, of future leaders of Maori and Native Hawaiian descent. The culturally sensitive students, the Fellows of the First Nations' Futures Program, spent a week at Kapalua Resort in 2007 to evaluate the adventure center and program. According to Teri Freitas Gorman, vice president of corporate communications for Maui Land & Pineapple Company, which hosted the First Nations' Fellows, the students "evaluated the land with nothing on it, and then with some preliminary plans, and then based upon our company values and theirs. They designed a plan outlining how we could use this as a resource for the Hawaiian community, the larger community, and how we could contribute to the environment rather than take away from it."

The Fellows highlighted the value of outdoor recreation as an educational and cultural experience. They recommended apprenticeships, educational field trips, and the involvement of children and elders in the community, as well as environmental measures, such as the planting of native trees, to minimize the carbon imprint. They also considered the possibility that medicinal plants might be identified in the mauka areas, which could then be made available to Native Hawaiian cultural practitioners, along with access to the area at no charge.

"We used those recommendations in planning the Mountain Outpost Experience," continued Gorman.

"As a result of their participation, it's much more soulful and thoughtful, with educational, cultural, and environmental components. This way, we are more conscious of the land, and rather than detracting from the environment, we can actually help to restore it."

Mutual aloha, as collaboration, is a part of the company's DNA, woven into its ethic and practices since Maui Land & Pineapple Company's inception. Colin Cameron until his death, and now Maui Land & Pineapple Company CEO David Cole, put that quality into action with regard to the environment, in their practice of conservation and conscious stewardship. The reverence for the land that Pu'u Kukui represents takes another form when applied internally, to the company's employees, many of whom brave housing challenges and long commutes to bring a level of efficiency to Kapalua Resort. "The travelers that Cole plans to attract like experiences that are authentic," wrote Paul Wood in *Hawaii* magazine in its January/February 2007 issue, "not just in terms of contact with nature but also in contact with people. They'll want to meet people who are actually from and of Hawaii. This provides Cole with the rationale for one of his most passionately felt strategies: 'attracting and retaining our local people, people who know this place and love it, especially people in their peak earning and child-bearing years.'" [2]

Pulelehua, a town within bicycling distance to Kapalua Resort, is one of Cole's solutions to the statewide "brain drain." After years of planning, hands-on community workshops, and input and feedback from local residents, the Maui Planning Commission approved Maui Land & Pineapple Company's development plans for Pulelehua. The plans call for 500 homes below market price—about seventy percent of the development—to be built in West Maui, in an attractive traditional neighborhood. Parks and open space, a town center, pedestrian-friendly streets, and an elementary school are some of the features of this new community for West Maui's working families.

In a letter to Kapalua homeowners, Cole described Pulelehua as a vital link in the company's overall plan to improve the hospitality experience in West Maui. "As a large landowner," he wrote, "our strategy is simple: to improve the quality of life for our employees by using our land to lower their cost of housing…It is therefore our duty to create an environment where all of us feel safe, healthy and secure."

A carefully planned, two-mile zipline course is part of the Mountain Outpost Experience.

Similarly, Maui Land & Pineapple Company provided considerable support, including scholarship funds, land, buildings, and infrastructure, to the fifteen-acre campus of Maui Preparatory Academy in Nāpili. West Maui's newest independent school, Maui Prep is a college preparatory school for pre-kindergarten through high school. Combined with the planned housing at Pulelehua, the school makes it possible for Maui Land & Pineapple Company to become the employer of choice in West Maui, said Cole. "Parents who care deeply about where their kids go to school are the best employees."

The creation of a new paradigm for living also entails alternate energy production, and toward this end, Maui Land & Pineapple Company, with partners Kamehameha Schools and Grove Farm, founded Hawai'i BioEnergy, designed to identify and develop renewable energy solutions for the state. Other partners include venture capitalist Vinod Khosla and Finistere Ventures.

"Working in concert with other renewable energy efforts, we can showcase Hawai'i as the world's leading example of how to live responsibly with abundant energy in the post-petroleum era," Cole told the Chamber of Commerce of Hawai'i in July 2006. He then proposed his version of Bhutan's well-publicized Gross National Happiness index: The Aloha Wealth Index. Hawai'i's long-term well-being and prosperity, he suggested, could be measured in economic, environmental, and cultural terms. In the environmental category, the Aloha

Wealth Index would be determined by such benchmarks as restored near-shore fisheries, the percentage of protected versus developed land, the acreage of healthy native forests, the number of humpback whales born in island waters, and the percentage of energy that is renewable. Cultural yardsticks, in Cole's estimation, would be the percentage of one-year-olds celebrating with baby lū'au (traditional Hawaiian feasts), the ratio of island-grown over imported food, the number of children in hula hālau, and the acres of taro under cultivation. These are significant cultural symbols that hark back to a time when Hawai'i had greater self-sufficiency.

Holistic planning at this level is not just talk, but ideas in action, with results that may not always be expressible, but are palpable. Ask George Mackin, who joyfully paints his canvas of life every day he's in West Maui. Or Ginger Prince, the longtime manager of Honolua Store, who considers her employees her "extended family." Prince recycles the trash, picks up debris from the roadside, and quietly thinks about "where the world should be going.

"When I'm working at the store and someone comes in, the greeting is sincere," she commented. "It's easy to be sincere when you love and care about a place. I've always felt that this resort has its own heart. It has its own beating heart, and everything around it comes from that place."

A lone surfer at Oneloa Bay takes in the fiery panorama.

Notes

--Ancient Murmurs

1 Some sources, such as Handy and Handy, *Native Planters*, 488, claim that the bays are named after Kiha-a-Piʻilani, Piʻilani's son, who continued Piʻilani's work in unification and public works.

2 Many who grew up in Honokahua call it Honokohua. There are several place names in the region that have different versions in popular use.

3 Kyselka and Lanterman, *Maui: How It Came to Be*, 62.

4 Kamakau, *Ruling Chiefs of Hawaii*, 348.

5 Kapalua Nui is a registered trademark of Maui Land & Pineapple Company.

6 The West Maui ahupuaʻa of Maui Land & Pineapple Company are Honokōhau, Honolua, Honokahua, Nāpili, Honokeana, ʻAlaeloa, Mailepai, Kahana, Māhinahina, and Moʻomuku.

7 Handy and Handy, *Native Planters*, 494.

8 Kyselka and Lanterman, *Maui: How It Came to Be*, 9. Kamakau, *Ruling Chiefs of Hawaii*, 61. Maui Nui a Kama refers to "Maui, land of Kama," a tribute to Kamalalawalu, the grandson of Piʻilani and son of Kiha-a-Piʻilani.

9 Moses Manu, "Ka Moolelo O Kihapiilani," *Ka Nupepa Kuokoa* (Aug. 23, 1884), quoted in Sterling, *Sites of Maui*, 53.

10 Kamakau, *Ruling Chiefs of Hawaii*, 74. Kamakau uses Honokawai instead of Honokōwai, which is the popular usage today.

11 According to Edna Pualani Farden Bekeart, a kamaʻaina and kupuna of Lahaina, Piʻilani Makua, the elder Piʻilani, began the trail but never finished. "He started it up here in northwest Maui, and he only took it from Lahaina to Kekaʻa," she notes. Piʻilani's son, Kiha-a-Piʻilani, finished the trail "and did all of the hard work." Personal interview with the author on September 26, 2007.

12 Handy and Handy, *Native Planters*, 490.

13 Ibid., 489.

14 Ibid.

15 Earl Kukahiko, the reverend's son, is among many who grew up in the area who refer to it as Honokohua.

16 Rosendahl and Rogers, *Archaeological Survey*, 3.

17 Ibid.

18 Ibid., 24.

19 Schmitt, *Missionary Censuses*, 190-191.

20 Donham, *Data Recovery*, 8.1.

21 Ibid., 2.3.

22 Ibid.

23 Jokiel, "Colin Cameron's Toughest Decision," 21.

ʻĀina Aloha

1 Akoni Akana, executive director of Friends of Mokuʻula, personal correspondence with the author, October 3, 2007. Akana notes that Mauna Kahalawai has also been called Kahalewai, "house of the water." Most places, said Akana, were named long before westerners arrived, and names may have been altered when recorded. Places in Hawaiʻi often have more than one name.

2 Liittschwager and Middleton, *Remains of a Rainbow*, 88.

3 Kyselka and Lanterman, *Maui: How It Came to Be*, 62.

4 Wexler, "Puʻu Kukui," 1.

5 Timmons, *Last Stand*.

6 Wexler, "Rare Garden," 43.

7 Ibid., 45.

8 Ibid., 43.

9 Ibid.

10 Pukui and Elbert, *Hawaiian Dictionary*, 389.

11 Akoni Akana, executive director of Friends of Mokuʻula, personal correspondence with the author, October 3, 2007.

12 Liittschwager and Middleton, *Remains of a Rainbow*, 85.

13 Fornander, *Hawaiian Antiquities*, 533-544.

The Bays of Piʻilani

1 Natives of the region often refer to the valley and bay as Honanana, as does Sterling in *Sites of Maui*, 46.

2 According to John and Michele Kern, who interviewed Maui ethnohistorian Inez Ashdown on August 19, 1976, "Mokuleia [sic] is where the red earth (*lepo alae*), used for dye, is found. It's in a cave there, and it's the only place on Maui that she knows of where one can get it, although there must be other places. It's near where the slaughterhouse stood on Piha Pt.," Maui Land & Pineapple Company archive.

3 John R. K. Clark interviewed by the author, September 9, 2007.

4 Pukui, *ʻŌlelo Noʻeau*, 89.

5 Bishop Museum Hawaiian Ethnobotany Online Database. *http://www2.bishopmuseum.org/ethnobotanydb/resultsdetailed.asp?search=ulei* (accessed November 13, 2007).

6 Pukui and Elbert, *Hawaiian Dictionary*, 296.

7 Handy and Handy, *Native Planters*, 495.

8 Wilson, "Maui Man," B-1.

9 Ibid.

Sam Kaʻai (Hōkūleʻa) sidebar, 51.

1 Benson, "Canoe May Sail," A-3.

2 Morse, "Stage Set for Voyage," 2.

The Land of Plenty

1 From an unknown writer, December 1914, Maui Land & Pineapple Company archive.

2 *Plantation Days*, 17.

3 Ibid.

4 Shigeto Nishimura interviewed by Shuji Seki, July 16, 1977, Maui Land & Pineapple Company archive.

5 Notes prepared by Paul Van Zwalenberg, July 2, 1983, Maui Land & Pineapple Company archive.

6 *Kapalua Nature Journal*, 1997-1998, 6-7.

[7] Baldwin Packers was incorporated in 1923, Maui Land & Pineapple Company records.

[8] Goldman, "Embracing the Past," 32.

[9] Harry Pali interviewed by Shuji Seki, September 9, 1977, Maui Land & Pineapple Company archive.

[10] Harry Pali interviewed by Lesley Bruce, June 12, 1978, Maui Land & Pineapple Company archive.

[11] Ibid.

[12] Ka'ai asserts that the valley is named Honokahau. Many local residents use place names that differ from formal literary or cartographic versions.

[13] Francis "Tito" Marciel interviewed by Lesley Bruce, June 14, 1978, Maui Land & Pineapple Company archive.

[14] Ibid.

[15] Bornhorst, "Beautiful, Useful Aloe," E-5.

[16] Shuji Seki interviewed by Dania Keane, June 29, 1984, Maui Land & Pineapple Company archive.

[17] *Plantation Days*, 19.

[18] Letter to Jack T. Waterhouse, April 2, 1946, courtesy of Maizie Sanford, sister of Colin Cameron.

[19] *Plantation Days*, 24.

H. P. Baldwin sidebar, 66.

[1] Baldwin, *A Memoir of Henry Perrine Baldwin*, 15.

[2] Royal Patent No. 2236, "Kamehameha to Kale Davis," November 22, 1855, Maui Land & Pineapple Company archive.

[3] Katherine Kama'ema'e Smith, on page 224 of her book *The Love Remains*, wrote: "When many Kapalua Resort homeowners look at a title search for their property, they will see Kale Davis noted as the earliest recorded owner of their land, granted to her in a Royal Patent of Confirmation in 1855 by King Kamehameha IV."

[4] From a research paper by Inez Ashdown, *Henry Perrine Baldwin*, 1973, 1, Maui Land & Pineapple Company archive.

[5] Baldwin, *A Memoir of Henry Perrine Baldwin*, 38.

[6] Ibid., 41.

Paradise Found

[1] Laurance Rockefeller to Colin C. Cameron, October 13, 1978, Maui Land & Pineapple Company archive.

[2] Colin Cameron interviewed by Nancy Markel of Hall & Levine Advertising, in Los Angeles, Fall 1974, 3, Maui Land & Pineapple Company archive.

[3] Jokiel, "Colin Cameron's Toughest Decision," 17.

[4] Colin Cameron interviewed by Nancy Markel of Hall & Levine Advertising, in Los Angeles, Fall 1974, 9, Maui Land & Pineapple Company archive.

[5] Maui Land & Pineapple Company, *http://www.mauiland.com/history.shtml* (accessed October 28, 2007).

[6] Bone, "Loli 'ana: Seeds of Transformation," 74.

[7] Colin Cameron interviewed by Nancy Markel of Hall & Levine Advertising, in Los Angeles, Fall 1974, 11, Maui Land & Pineapple Company archive.

[8] Pukui, Elbert, and Mookini, *Place Names of Hawaii*, 87.

[9] Maly, *Kapalua at Honokahua*, 3.

[10] Foster, "Which God Are We Waiting for?," 11.

[11] Jokiel, "The Saga of Kapalua," 26.

[12] Ibid.

[13] Yamanouchi, "New CEO ready," C-1.

[14] Eagar, "A New Future," A-1.

[15] Kubota, "Guests and Workers," A-5.

[16] Villano, "A Return to the Land."

Cornucopia

[1] David Cole, speech to the Hawai'i Business 2050 Forums on Sustainability, January 26, 2007.

[2] *Mālama 'āina* means "care for the land." Pukui and Elbert, *Hawaiian Dictionary*, 214.

[3] Petrini, "Communities of Food," 14.

The Global Village

[1] McDonough and Braungart, *Cradle to Cradle*, 183.

[2] Wood, "Fragile Island," 39.

Glossary

āholehole *Kuhlia sandvicensis*; young Hawaiian flagtail

ahupua'a traditional unit of land, usually stretching from mountain to sea

'āina land

alaloa a road that spans a lengthy distance

ali'i chief; member of the royal class

'amakihi *Loxops virens*; native yellow/greenish honey creeper

'a'o *Puffinus puffinis newelli*; Newell's shearwater

'apapane *Himatione sanguinea*; native crimson/black honey creeper

'aumakua family guardian spirit

'awa *Piper methysticum*; a Polynesian-introduced plant used in ritual and for medicine

'āwiwi *Centaurium sebaeoides*; an endangered Hawaiian herb

'ele'ele or *limu 'ele'ele* *Enteromorpha prolifera*; an edible green seaweed

hāhā *Cyanea lobata/Cyanea magnicalyx*; endangered Hawaiian plants, bellflower family

ha'iwale, kanawao ke'oke'o *Cyrtandra munroi*; a rare Hawaiian shrub, African violet family

hala *Pandanus tectorius*; an indigenous tree whose leaves are traditionally woven into mats and other household objects

halakahiki pineapple

haole koa *Leucaena leucocephala*; an introduced weedy shrub

hāpu'u *Cibotium chamissoi*; a Hawaiian tree fern

hau *Hibiscus tiliaceus*; a Polynesian-introduced tree used for canoe outriggers, rope, and medicine

he'e octopus

heiau ancient place of worship

Hesperomannia arborescens an endangered Hawaiian shrub or small tree in the sunflower family; no known Hawaiian name

honu turtle

i'e kuku bark-cloth beater

'i'iwi *Vestiaria coccinea*; scarlet Hawaiian honey creeper

'iliahialo'e *Santalum ellipticum*; Hawaiian coast sandalwood shrub or small tree

imu underground oven

ipu a gourd, often used as a container

iwi bone

kahu 'āina a land steward; one who oversees landed resources

kalo *Colocasia esculenta*; the staple starch of the Hawaiian people

kālua a cooking technique of roasting food underground

kama'āina a "child of the land" or a long-term resident

kani ka pū "the conch shell sounds"

kapa a cloth made from the bark of fibrous plants

kapu sacred, restricted rights and privileges

ki'i a sacred image, carved or made of feathers

kīpapa paved or cobbled

koli'i *Trematolobelia macrostachys*; an uncommon Hawaiian shrub in the bellflower family, now only known on O'ahu and Maui

Kona southerly winds and rains; districts to the south

kūkini a runner or a messenger

kukui *Aleurites moluccana*; Polynesian-introduced candlenut tree; state tree of Hawai'i

kuleana responsibility, right, property

kumu source of knowledge, teacher

kūpuna elders, grandparents

lauhala leaf of the pandanus tree used in weaving

lei niho palaoa chiefly symbol of rank, made of a carved whale's tooth pendant hung on an intricately woven hair necklace

liliwai *Acaena exigua*; a small, endangered native herb in the rose family, growing only in the bogs of Pu'u Kukui, West Maui, and Mt. Wai'ale'ale, Kaua'i

limu seaweed

limu kala *Sargassum echinocarpum*; a tough though edible brown seaweed used in rituals

limu kohu *Asparagopsis taxiformis*; a very popular edible seaweed eaten with seafood

limu pepe'e or *līpe'epe'e* *Laurencia parvipapillata*; an edible red seaweed

lo'i an irrigated terrace for taro cultivation

lū'au a Hawaiian feast

Lydgate's Pteris fern *Pteris lydgatei*; endangered on Maui and believed to be extinct on Moloka'i; no known Hawaiian name

māhoe, 'ala'alahua *Alectryon macrococcus*; an endangered Hawaiian tree

mai'a momona "sweet banana"

makani wind

mālama i ka 'āina to care for or preserve the land

mana a spiritual essence or life force

mauka inland, upland

milo *Thespesia populnea*; a native shoreline tree whose wood is prized for carving

mochi Japanese pounded rice cake

moi *Polydactylus sexfilis*; a thread fish much desired for eating, especially by chiefs

moku a district comprised of individual ahupua'a

mo'o a water spirit having a lizard-like form

naupaka kahakai, naupaka kuahiwi *Scaevola* spp.; a shrub that grows both along the shore (kahakai) and in the uplands (kuahiwi), recognizable for its white or yellow half-flower

'ohana family, both immediate and extended

'ōhi'a *Metrosideros polymorpha*; a Hawaiian tree having red blossoms sacred to the volcano goddess

'ono delicious, tasty

'ōpae shrimp

'ōpe'ape'a starfish, or the Hawaiian bat

'opihi limpet, a shellfish

pali cliff

paniolo cowboy

pauoa Ctenitis squamigera; an endangered Hawaiian fern

pā'ū-o-Hi'iaka Jacquemontia ovalifolia sandwicensis; a native shoreline vine

pu'e Lobelia gloria-montis; the Glory of the Mountain; a rare Hawaiian plant growing only in the montane bogs of Maui and Moloka'i

pueo Asio flammeus sandwichensis; Hawaiian short-eared owl (in other entries it is sandwicensis and sandvicensis)

puhi eel

sumo Japanese wrestling

ua rain

'ua'u Pterodroma phaeopygia sandwichensis; the Hawaiian petrel, an endangered seabird

'ua'u kani Puffinus pacificus chlororhynchus; wedge-tailed shearwater

'ulu breadfruit

uluhe, unuhe Dicranopteris linearis; false staghorn

u'ulei, 'ūlei Osteomeles anthyllidifolia; a native woody shrub in the rose family used to make 'ō'ō, or digging sticks, fish spears, and a musical instrument, the 'ukēkē

wana Diadema paucispinum; sea urchin

wao akua upland mountainous regions inhabited by gods and spirits

wauke Broussonetia papyrifera; paper mulberry whose bark is used to make Hawaiian kapa/tapa cloth

People and Places

Alapa'i Nui ancient chief of Hawai'i

'Au'au channel between Maui and Lāna'i

'E'eke or 'Eke crater and peak in West Maui

Ha'ikū a land area in East Maui

Hālau o Lauhuki me La'ahana the name of a hālau dedicated to the patron goddess of kapa

Haleakalā "House of the Sun," a prominent crater in East Maui and the tallest volcano on Maui

Hāna a coastal area in East Maui

Hi'iaka-i-ka-poli-o-Pele younger sister of Pele

Hōkūle'a a navigational star, possibly Arcturus; a voyaging double-hulled canoe was named for this star

Honokahua an ahupua'a in West Maui

Honokeana an ahupua'a in West Maui

Honokōhau an ahupua'a in West Maui

Honokōwai an ahupua'a in West Maui

Honolua an ahupua'a in West Maui

Hononana an ahupua'a in West Maui; also referred to as Honanana by local residents

'Īao stream, valley, and peak in Wailuku district

'Ili'ilikea an ancient temple in northwest Maui

Kā'anapali a district in West Maui noted for its beaches and resorts

Kahakuloa a remote land area in northwest Maui

Kahana land area in West Maui

Kahauiki land area in northwest Maui

Kaho'olawe island to the west of Maui, formerly set aside for military use

Kamehameha Hawaiian chief who united the various islands under his sovereign control

Kamehameha-nui ancient chief who ruled on Maui; the son of Kekaulike

Kapalua Nui all of ML&P's land holdings in West Maui, including the Kapalua Resort

Ka'ū a district in the southern part of the island of Hawai'i

Kaupō a large land area in East Maui

Kiha-a-Pi'ilani son of chief Pi'ilani

Kihawahine a powerful water spirit revered by many chiefs

Ki'owaiokiha "fresh water pool of Kiha"

Lahaina former capital of Hawai'i where chiefs resided

Lahainaluna upland area where the first school west of the Rockies was established in 1831

Lāna'i island southwest of Maui

Līhau a mountain in Lahaina district

Māhinahina land area and ahupua'a in West Maui

Mailepai land area and ahupua'a in West Maui

Maiu an ancient temple in northwest Maui

Mālā land area and port in Lahaina

Mauna Kahalawai West Maui mountain range

Mokulē'ia a beach and bay in northwest Maui that are part of a marine preserve

Moloka'i island between Maui and O'ahu

Molokini islet between Maui and Kaho'olawe

Nā Hono-a-Pi'ilani "The Bays of Pi'ilani;" a reference to the bays of West Maui, particularly those whose names begin with the prefix "Hono-"

Nākālele the northernmost point of land on Maui, famous for its blow-hole

Nāpali "The Cliffs"

Nāpili bay and land area in West Maui

Nāpilihau land area in West Maui

Pailolo channel between Maui and Moloka'i

Pele volcano goddess

Pele-io-holani chief of O'ahu

Poelua a bay and gulch in Kahakuloa

Pu'u Kukui "Hill of Light/Enlightenment;" a peak famous for being West Maui's highest point at 5,788 feet above sea level

Pu'ulaina a hill in Lahaina district

Waialua land area in Hālawa, district on Moloka'i

Bibliography

Ashdown, Inez MacPhee. *Ke Alaloa o Maui*. Wailuku, HI: Kama'aina Historians, Inc., 1971.

Baldwin, Arthur D. *A Memoir of Henry Perrine Baldwin, 1842 to 1911*. Cleveland, OH: Privately printed, 1915.

Bartholomew, Gail. *Maui Remembers: A Local History*. Photo research by Bren Bailey. Honolulu: Mutual Publishing, 1994.

Benson, Bruce. "Canoe May Sail Today for Tahiti." *Honolulu Advertiser*, May 1, 1976, A-3.

Bone, Robert W. "Loli'ana: Seeds of Transformation." *Hawai'i ka 'oihana hokele, the History of Hawai'i's Hotel Industry, 1840s to 1990*. Special commemorative edition of *Hawaiian Hospitality*, 1990, 50-74.

Bornhorst, Heidi. "Beautiful, Useful Aloe Is a Gift from Africa." *Honolulu Advertiser*, May 25, 2007, E-5.

Clark, John R. K. *The Beaches of Maui County*. Honolulu: University Press of Hawaii, 1980.

Desha, Stephen L. *Kamehameha and his Warrior Kekūhaupi'o*. Translated by Frances N. Frazier. Honolulu: Kamehameha Schools Press, 2000.

Donham, Theresa K. "Data Recovery Excavations at the Honokahua Burial Site, Land of Honokahua, Lahaina District, Island of Maui." Prepared for Kapalua Land Company, Ltd. Hilo, HI: Paul H. Rosendahl, Ph.D., Inc., 2000.

Eagar, Harry. "A New Future for ML&P." *Maui News*, March 26, 2004, A-1.

Finney, Ben R. *Voyage of Rediscovery: A Cultural Odyssey through Polynesia*. In collaboration with Marlene Among et al. Illustrations by Richard Rhodes. Berkeley and Los Angeles: University of California Press, 1994.

Fornander, Abraham. H*awaiian Antiquities and Folk-lore*. 1918. Volume V. Reprint. Honolulu: Bishop Museum Press, 2004.

Foster, Jeanette. "Which God Are We Waiting for?...or … Breaking Ground at Kapalua." *Maui Sun*, February 23–March 1, 1977, 11.

Fujii, Jocelyn. *In the Lee of Hualalai: Historic Ka'ūpūlehu*. Photography by Franco Salmoiraghi; introduction by Hannah Kihalani Springer. Kailua-Kona, HI: Ka'ūpūlehu Makai Venture, 1995.

Goldman, Rita. "Embracing the Past." *Embrace* (Kapalua), 2005, 32.

Gutmanis, June. *Na Pule Kahiko: Ancient Hawaiian Prayers*. Drawings by Susanne Indich. Honolulu: Editions Limited, 1983.

Handy, E. S. Craighill, and Elizabeth Green Handy. *Native Planters in Old Hawaii: Their Life, Lore and Environment*. Honolulu: Bishop Museum Press, 1972.

Hawaii Audubon Society. *Hawaii's Birds*. 4th ed. Honolulu: The Society, 1993.

Honolulu Advertiser. "Hokule'a at Maui—Next Stop Tahiti." April 27, 1976, A-3.

Honolulu Star-Bulletin. "Hokule'a Completes First Leg of Trip." April 26, 2007, A-1.

Ii, John Papa. *Fragments of Hawaiian History*. Translated by Mary Kawena Pukui. Edited by Dorothy B. Barrère. Honolulu: Bishop Museum Press, 1959.

James, Van. *Ancient Sites of Maui, Moloka'i and Lāna'i: Archaeological Places of Interest in the Hawaiian Islands*. Honolulu: Mutual Publishing, 2002.

Joesting, Ann. *Historical Research for the Makena-Keoneoio Road in Makena, Maui*. Honolulu: Bishop Museum, 1986.

Jokiel, Lucy. "Colin Cameron's Toughest Decision." *Hawaii Business*, May 1989, 16-28.

————. "The Saga of Kapalua." *Hawaii Business*, May 1989, 26-27.

Kamakau, Samuel Mānaikalani. *Ka po'e kahiko: the People of Old*. Translated from the newspaper *Ke au 'oko'a* by Mary Kawena Pukui; arranged and edited by Dorothy B. Barrère; illustrated by Joseph Feher. Honolulu: Bishop Museum Press, 1964.

————. *Ruling Chiefs of Hawai'i*. Honolulu: Kamehameha Schools Press, 1992.

————. *Tales and Traditions of the People of Old: Nā Mo'olelo a ka Po'e Kahiko*. Translated from the newspapers *Ka Nupepa Kuokoa* and *Ke Au Okao* by Mary Kawena Pukui; edited by Dorothy B. Barrère. Honolulu: Bishop Museum Press, 1991.

Kame'eleihiwa, Lilikalā. *Native Land and Foreign Desires: Pehea lā e pono ai?* Honolulu: Bishop Museum Press, 1992.

Kāne, Herb Kawainui. *Voyager: Words and Images*. Design by Robert B. Goodman and Herb Kawainui Kane; text edition by Paul Berry; managing editor, Robert B. Goodman and Lorie Rapkin. Bellevue, WA: Whalesong Inc., 1991.

Kern, John, and Michele Kern. "Proposal for a Natural Hawaiian Natural History Botanic Garden at Honokahua." Unpublished report. West Maui, HI: Maui Land & Pineapple Company, 1975.

Kubota, Gary. "Guests and Workers Say Aloha." *Honolulu Advertiser,* April 8, 2006, A-5.

Kyselka, Will, and Ray Lanterman. *Maui: How It Came to Be.* Honolulu: University Press of Hawaii, 1980.

Landgraf, Anne Kapulani. *Na Wahi Kapu o Maui.* Introduction by Kīhei De Silva. Honolulu: 'Ai Pohaku Press, 2003.

Liittschwager, David, and Susan Middleton. *Remains of a Rainbow: Rare Plants and Animals of Hawai'i.* Foreword by W. S. Merwin. Washington, D.C.: National Geographic Society, 2001.

Malo, David. *Hawaiian Antiquities.* 2nd ed. Translated from the Hawaiian by Dr. N. B. Emerson. Honolulu: Bishop Museum Press, 1971.

Maly, Kepā. "Kapalua at Honokahua, Kā'anapali Lahaina District, Island of Maui. A History of Place Name Occurrences in Archival Records." TMK Overview Sheet 2-4-02. Lāna'i City, HI: Kumu Pono Associates, LLC.

McDonough, William, and Michael Braungart. *Cradle to Cradle: Remaking the Way We Make Things.* New York: North Point Press, 2002.

McKinzie, Edith Kawelohea. *Hawaiian Genealogies.* Edited by Ishmael W. Stagner II. Vol. 2. Lā'ie, HI: Brigham Young and the Polynesian Cultural Center, 2003.

Morse, Stephen K. *Voyage of Rediscovery, Hōkūle'a '85-87: A Cultural, Educational, and Scientific Expedition.* Honolulu: Special Events Hawaii, n.d.

Nakuina, Moses K. *The Wind Gourd of La'amaomao: the Hawaiian Story of Pāka'a and Kūapāka'a, Personal Attendants of Keawenuiaumi, Ruling Chief of Hawaii and Descendants of La'amaomao.* Collected, edited, and expanded by Moses K. Nakuina; translated by Esther T. Mookini and Sarah Nākoa. Honolulu: Kalamakū Press, 1992.

Plantation Days, Remembering Honolua. Consultants Inez Ashdown et al.; edited by Effie Cameron and D. E. Keane. Kahului, HI: Maui Land & Pineapple Company, 1987.

Pukui, Mary Kawena, and Samuel H. Elbert. *Hawaiian Dictionary.* Honolulu: University Press of Hawaii, 1971.

Pukui, Mary Kawena. *'Ōlelo No'eau: Hawaiian Proverbs and Poetical Sayings.* Collected, translated, and annotated by Mary Kawena Pukui; illustrated by Dietrich Varez. Honolulu: Bishop Museum Press, 1983.

Pukui, Mary Kawena, Samuel H. Elbert, and Esther T. Mookini. *Place Names of Hawaii.* Honolulu: University Press of Hawaii, 1974.

Rosendahl, Paul, and Donnell J. Rogers. "Archaeological Survey and Recording Iliilikea and Maiu Heiau on the North Coast of Maui." Prepared for Kapalua Land Company, Ltd. Hilo, HI: Paul H. Rosendahl, Ph.D., Inc., 1992.

Schmitt, Robert C. *The Missionary Censuses of Hawaii.* Pacific Anthropological Records 20. Honolulu: Dept. of Anthropology, Bernice Pauahi Bishop Museum, 1973.

Smith, Katherine Kama'ema'e. *The Love Remains.* South Bend, IN, and Maui, HI: Honu Publications, 2005.

Sterling, Elspeth P., comp. *Sites of Maui.* Honolulu: Bishop Museum Press, 1998.

Timmons, Grady. *Last Stand.* Arlington, VA: The Nature Conservancy, 2003.

Tong, David. "Hokule'a Bids Aloha to Oahu, Well-Wishers." *Honolulu Advertiser,* April 26, 1976, A-5.

University of Hawai'i at Hilo. Dept. of Geography. *Atlas of Hawai'i.* 3rd ed. Edited by Sonia P. Juvik and James O. Juvik. Chief cartographer, Thomas R. Paradise. Honolulu: University of Hawaii Press, 1998.

Villano, Matt. "A Return to the Land, for Fuel." *New York Times,* May 19, 2007.

Wexler, Mark. "Pu'u Kukui, Hill of Enlightenment." *Kapalua Nature Journal,* Summer/Fall 2000, 1.

———. "Rare Garden in the Realm of the Gods." *National Wildlife,* 35, no. 3, April-May 1997, 40.

Wilson, Christie. "Maui Man, 74, Saves Seabird Colony." *Honolulu Advertiser,* March 14, 2007, B-1.

Wood, Paul. "Fragile Island." *Hawaii,* January/February 2007, 39.

Yamanouchi, Kelly. "New CEO Ready to Revamp Maui Land." *Honolulu Advertiser,* September 10, 2003.

Youngblood, Ron. *On the Hana Coast.* Produced and directed by Leonard Lueras. Hong Kong: Emphasis International, 1992.

Acknowledgments

A multitude of blessings informed this book: a fascinating subject, the extensive and impeccably preserved archives of Maui Land & Pineapple Company, and, most importantly, the assistance and support of those who know the area and were generous enough to share their stories.

Carol Silva, writer, researcher, and archivist with the Hawai'i State Archives, joined me in researching Hawaiian documents and was invaluable in translating old Hawaiian texts and helping me flesh out the otherwise spotty history of northwest Maui. With her sharp memory and keen eye, Eunice Garcia, keeper of the ML&P archives, spent long hours sifting through files to help me discover the more arcane details of the company's history. Many thanks also to Sylvia Hunt, formerly the records management director of Maui Land & Pineapple Company, who momentarily left a happy retirement to answer my pleas for help.

Clifford Nae'ole, cultural adviser for The Ritz-Carlton, Kapalua, was an ally from the beginning. He led me to people with deep ties to the area and assisted me in many aspects of preparation. Clifford led me to Pi'imauna 'Aiwohi, a descendant of Hawaiians who lived at Honokahua before The Ritz-Carlton, Kapalua was built. In honor of her ancestors, Pi'imauna composed the chant that opens this book and was kind enough to let us publish it. Silla Kaina, cultural resources coordinator for Kapalua Land Company, and her mother, Orpha Kaina, were also major contributors to this effort. They extended their hospitality to me and taught me more about Hawaiian wisdom than can be expressed in words or learned in books. Kiha Kaina, Orpha's grandson, is knowledgeable beyond his years and was generous in sharing his insights.

Pua Van Dorpe, the awe-inspiring (and modest) master of kapa-making, is an essential part of Kapalua's cultural history for having spearheaded the kapa-making for the reburials at Kapalua. I witnessed her strength and devotion as she gathered the women of the hālau for the daunting task some twenty years ago. I am indebted to her and Bob Van Dorpe for their contribution to this book, and for their lifelong commitment to the cultural life of Hawai'i. Kepā Maly, ever gracious, was a major cultural resource, sharing information and the results of research he conducted on the area years ago. Akoni Akana was infinitely knowledgeable, with obscure facts and sources at the ready, a scholar and activist in the most honorable sense of the word. Edna Pualani Farden Bekeart, esteemed kupuna and devoted researcher of the Pi'ilani line, offered facts, observations, and opinions from her many years of living and teaching in Lahaina. Sam Ka'ai, an old friend with ties to this region, was generous with his time and *mana'o* (thoughts) and is invariably a fount of cultural information, as well as a raconteur extraordinaire. Randy Bartlett shared not only his treasure trove of information about Pu'u Kukui, but also some excellent photos that he has taken through the years. His photos of the *'ua'u kani* (wedge-tailed shearwater) chicks in "The Bays of Pi'ilani" chapter are among those we proudly unveil in these pages. Wes Nohara, who is the third generation with roots in Honolua, was a wonderful resource on plantation life and agriculture, and I am indebted to him for his presence in this book.

Many others helped, some mentioned in these pages and others behind the scenes. Alphabetically, they are: Caroline Belsom, Tova Callender, Wayne Carroll, Ryan Churchill, Charlie Dofa, Chico Gomes, Val Ho'opai, Estellita Kaiser, Charles Ka'upu, Earl Kukahiko, George Mackin, Henrietta Mahuna, Isao Nakagawa, Lehua and Aimoku Pali, Nate Smith, and Megan Webster. A special thanks to Maizie Sanford and Richard Cameron, the sister and son of Colin Cameron.

I thank also David Watersun, who took most of the photographs in the book, and Daphne Chu, Merriam Fontanilla, and Arikka Johnson of Ostrander-Chu, Inc., whose graphic talents are showcased in these pages. Special thanks to Franco Salmoiraghi, whose black-and-white photo accompanies the sidebar of Pua Van Dorpe. Mapmaker Bill Horak was a delight to work with; his integrity and skills perfectly matched our intentions. His archival maps are thoughtfully researched and respectfully executed, and we are proud to be the first to publish his work.

Those most aware of what it takes to make a book are my editorial and publishing team. I thank them for their commitment, good humor, support, and skills. Dawn Sueoka, my editor, copyeditor, and proofreader, has worked with me on three books now, and, I hope, will be with me for many more. High pressure, long hours, and equanimity are an unlikely combination, but she is the rare professional who handles every challenge with aplomb. So it is with Sandra Acuna, the miracle indexer who continues to organize the back matter of my books with laser-sharp instincts and the consummate skills of an advanced librarian with global skills.

At Hula Moon Press, business manager Linda Taketa and print production manager Barbara Grange shepherded this book from its embryonic stage to its full unveiling. It was a demanding, fun, occasionally manic, and always entertaining process, spiked with the generous dollops of humor that have always been our saving grace. Mahalo to the Hula Moon team.

Finally, a tip of the hat to those at Maui Land & Pineapple Company who made this book possible. Teri Gorman and Karin Sagar were the ideal partners who opened the doors of possibility and saw this book through to completion. Teri and Karin worked closely with me every step of the way and never wavered in their expressions of confidence. Thank you also to Karen Thompson for her expert touches on design.

To David and Maggie Cole, a resounding mahalo a nui loa. Good, caring people with a solid vision and a plan for achievable action are rare in this world, and the opportunity to flesh out that vision in words is rarer still. After writing this book and delving into the macro- and micro-view of The World According to Cole, I am bolstered, personally and professionally, by the prospect of a brighter world, a more hopeful future, for these islands that we love so deeply.

To Bradley Shields: thank you, always, for being the space between the words.

Jocelyn Fujii

Index

Page numbers in italics refer to captions.

Credits

Photos, listed alphabetically:
Bob Bangerter: cover, 32 upper left, 34, 35, 49, 70-71, 78-79, 96, 97.
Randy Bartlett: 31, 32 upper right, 48 left and right.
David Boynton: 37.
Steve Brinkman: 87 lower left and upper right.
Ann Cecil: 83.
John De Mello: 14.
Thayer Jacoby: 16.
Ray Mains: 12-13, 88-89.
Bob McNatt: 36 left.
Tony Novak-Clifford: 28, 32 lower right, 90.
Hank Oppenheimer: 36 right.
Ethan Romanchak: 32 lower left.
Franco Salmoiraghi: 23.
John Severson: 26-27, 94.
David Watersun: 1, 2, 6, 10, 19-22, 24, 25, 33, 38-46, 50 right, 51-57, 61, 62, 66, 67, 69, 72, 77, 80, 82, 84, 86, 93, 98.
Ben Young: 50 (courtesy of the Polynesian Voyaging Society).

Design: Ostrander-Chu, Inc.
Cartography: William Horak, horakbbt@comcast.net
Editing, copy editing, and proof reading: Dawn Sueoka
Hawaiian translation, research, and editing: Carol Silva
Index: Sandra Acuna
Production and print management: Barbara Grange, The Print Connection Hawai'i LLC

MAUI
A
KAMA

Kai o Pailolo

KĀ'ANAPALI

WAILUKU

MAUNA

Mauna 'Eke

Pu'u
Kukui

Awāwa o 'Iao

Kūono
o Kahului

HĀMĀKUA
POKO

HĀMĀKUALOA

Moana Pākīpika 'Ākau

Ko'olau

Komohana   'Ākau   Hikina
              Hema

LAHAINĀ

KAHAKULOA

Kai o 'Au'au

Kūono
o Mā'alaea

KULA

MAKAWAO

Awāwa o Ke'anae

HĀNA

MAUNA

Awāwa o Koʻolau

HONUA'ULA

MOLOKINI

HALEAKALĀ

Kāwaha o Kaupō

KĪPAHULU

Kai o Kealaikahiki

Kai o 'Alalākeiki

KAHIKINUI

KAUPŌ

Kai o 'Alenuihāhā

William Horak October 2007